PIRATES AND BURIED
TREASURE
ON FLORIDA ISLANDS

While it's an undisputed fact that pirates, buccaneers, and plunderers once roamed the waters and shores of Florida, the stories in this book are a mixture of historic fact, myth, and fabrication. Serious historians don't accept the exploits attributed to José Gaspar as being true and accurate, and many even deny that he existed at all.

Author Jack Beater collected these pirate tales for their romance, fantasy, and adventure; readers should not accept them as historical fact nor as an aid to treasure hunting. As Beater himself admitted, "you can make a lot more out of pirate treasure by writing about it than you can by digging for it."

PIRATES AND BURIED
TREASURE
ON FLORIDA ISLANDS

including

The Gasparilla Story

by Jack Beater

A Great Outdoors Book

Great Outdoors Publishing Company
St. Petersburg, Florida

Manufactured in the United States of America

About the Author

JACK BEATER

JACK BEATER, the author of many books and short stories covering numerous facets of the Florida scene, was born in Philadelphia, Pennsylvania, just before the turn of the century. After living in Missouri, California, New Jersey, Cuba, and for seven years in Mexico City, he graduated from Penn State University in time to join the Army and serve in the First World War. In 1920, he came to South Florida for a two week visit.

Jack was so fascinated by the pirate stories he heard that his Florida vacation lasted for the rest of his life, as he went around asking every old codger he met for any stories that had been passed down from grandfather to father to son. He interviewed Florida settlers, writing down the tales they told him. Maybe they made them up. Maybe their grandfathers made them up. Or maybe they were the gospel truth—who knows?

A businessman for many years, Jack eventually made writing his full-time career, publishing many books and articles. He and his wife were residents of Fort Myers until his death in 1969.

CONTENTS

Gasparilla, the Pirate of Boca Grande 7

Juan Gomez, the Pirate of Panther Key 17

Captiva, Once an Isle of Captive Women 23

The Pirate and the Golden Haired Virgin 27

Honeymooners of Estero Island 39

The Black Pirate of Sanibel Island 45

Treasure at Key Largo 51

On the Trail of Pirate Treasure 57

Treasure — Thirty Fathoms Deep 65

The Missing Gold of Useppa Island 73

Treasure's Where You Find It 77

The Curse of Cara Pelau 83

The Yellow Gold of Black Island 89

The Capture of the MARY ANDERS 103

When Pirates Roamed Pine Island Sound 111

List of Atrocious Piracies and Barbarities 115

Foreword

I have been close to the Gasparilla story for almost 50 years. I first heard a part of Jose' Gaspar's life story from the lips of a young Cuban who was a fellow passenger on a steamer bound for Havana and Vera Cruz in 1911.

In later years I heard other parts of this pirate's life and deeds from some of the original American settlers of South Florida.

In addition I located much written material from the back files of magazines and books going back as far as 1823.

I also gratefully acknowledge the aid given me by Mr. E. D. Lambright, the editorial director of the Tampa Tribune.

The following brief story of Gasparilla's life is a condensation of several of the biographies I have written on this interesting buccaneer. The first published under the title of *The Story of Gasparilla*, was copyrighted in 1949. The second, and a longer version, was published under the title of *The Gasparilla Story*, in 1952 and 1956, and a full-length historical novel, *The Sea Avenger* was published by Dell in 1958.

The memory of Jose' Gaspar, or "Gasparilla", is perpetuated year after year by Ye Mystic Krewe of Gasparilla, a society of Tampa business and professional men, who sail into port every February and capture the City of Tampa. There follows a huge parade, the Pirates' Ball, and a week-long celebration. Ye Mystic Krewe of Gasparilla was organized in 1904, and in popular appeal Gasparilla week is surpassed only by the New Orleans Mardi Gras.

Gasparilla, guarded by Leon Gaspar, prepare to hide treasure
on Josefa's Island

Gasparilla, the Pirate of Boca Grande

Time: 1756 - 1821   *Place*: *Florida West Coast*

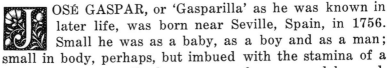OSÉ GASPAR, or 'Gasparilla' as he was known in later life, was born near Seville, Spain, in 1756. Small he was as a baby, as a boy and as a man; small in body, perhaps, but imbued with the stamina of a Spanish fighting bull, the courage of a cornered leopard, and the cunning of a black fox. He was kind to his friends, dangerous to his enemies, and always true to his word.

It is highly possible that Jose' Gaspar had much to do with Florida becoming a part of the Union, for if he had not settled on the Florida West Coast and become a thorn in the side of Spanish commerce with Cuba and Mexico, Spain might not have been willing to sell Florida to the United States. On the other hand the United States desired to control Florida and rid the surrounding waters of the pirates who molested shipping bound to or from the ports of Mobile and New Orleans.

Jose's parents belonged to the minor aristrocracy of Spain, being neither wealthy nor poor, and he was educated in what we would consider to be middle class surroundings. His smart little mind absorbed knowledge like a sponge, and his vivid imagination concocted impossible stories, and conceived fantastic plans. In his tiny sailboat he visited ships in the harbor, and listened to tall tales of slave ships, pirates, gold, women, and all the supposed wonders of the New World. There is little doubt but what these sailormen's tales did much to fill his mind with the lust for adventure.

At the age of twelve he kidnapped a neighbor's daughter and tried to collect ransom. The judge gave him a choice of going to the Spanish naval academy, or going to prison. As might be expected he chose the Royal Academy of Navigation, and spent the next six years years in learning the ways of ships and men. Little is known of his life during these years save that he was soon a master with sword or pistol, and had succeeded in being blamed for the seduction of the *commandante's* neice.

According to old records in the Spanish archives Don Jose' Gaspar's rise in the Navy of His Majesty, King Charles III, was little short of spectacular. One of his first acts as a lowly midshipman, was to swim into the harbor at Tripoli with a few chosen men, and recapture a Spanish merchantman the Tripolitan pirates were holding for ransom. A few years later, as captain of his own ship-of-war, he attacked a pirate stronghold on a Caribbean island, and carried the prisoners into Havana to be hung. One of the old records state: "In the year 1782, at the young age of twenty-six, Don Jose' Gaspar was promoted to the rank of *almirante* (admiral) of the Middle Atlantic Squadron."

Shortly after, the young Admiral was chosen by the Navy Minister to be the Navy's liason officer at the Royal Court in Madrid. History records show that he shone like a newly minted piece-of-eight against the jaded and stuffy atmosphere of the Court of King Charles III. His manners were in the best tradition, and his wit was filled with dash and sparkle. He was also — if we are to read between the lines — a past master at the art of love making.

In any case Maria Louisa, the Sicilian wife of the Crown Prince, soon became fond of the young and talented officer — in fact much too fond if the truth must be told. When he rejected her affections in order to give his true love to a beautiful lady-in-waiting, Maria Louisa and the Prime Minister, Manuel de Godoy, formed an alliance against him.

The plot the unholy pair hatched up made it appear that Don Jose' had been untrue to the King's trust, and had stolen some of the Royal jewels for his own personal gain. Charles III was taken in by the false evidence presented to him, and issued orders for Don Jose's immediate arrest.

Learning of his peril in time, and with a murderous desire for revenge, Jose' escaped to the coast and, with the aid of some escaped convicts, managed to capture a well found navy bark at the quayside, and put out to sea. At his urging his motley crew voted to become pirates, and a pirate with a hate against Spain Jose' Gaspar remained for the rest of his life.

As the undisputed head of his pirating venture, Gasparilla, as he was now known, sailed westward to cruise the Caribbean and prey upon Spanish ships and Spanish towns. In the next few years he captured many a valuable prize. The exact number will never be known, but Gasparilla's personal diary came into the possession of the Spanish authorities in 1795, and up to that time he had written down the names and loot secured, from 36 Spanish vessels he had captured and burned. He continued to make war upon Spanish holdings for another 26 years, and the total number of his prizes, and the humans he murdered must have been large.

As soon as a ship was captured the male prisoners were

herded into the bow of the ship, and any women and children into the stern. If in need of replacements for his own crew Gasparilla would single out likely men and offer them a chance for their life. The rest were dragged to the rail, knifed in the back, and tossed over the side.

Many of the female prisoners who fell into Gasparilla's hands fared as badly as the men. Some fared even worse. Those who were old, ugly or infirm were tossed to the sharks without waste of time. Children, in nearly every case, met the same fate. Those women whom Gasparilla allowed to live were divided among officers and crew, except those who were the wives or daughters of wealthy families, and who could be expected to bring a rich reward in gold. These women were treated with reasonable respect, and after the ransom money had been received they were set afoot on the shores of Cuba, Hispaniola or Puerto Rico.

An old story tells us that, "Gasparilla was a man of sudden rage, and retaliated by the letting of blood. On one occasion a Spanish maid of good family spit in his face when he tried to remove the golden rings from her ears. Gasparilla then ordered her head to be bound to a mast by the long braids of her hair, after which he took his sword and sliced off both her ears in order to secure the trinkets without further insult to himself."

Gasparilla operated in the Caribbean and Gulf of Mexico at a time in history when conditions favored piracy on the high seas. Spanish strength was at its lowest ebb, the new Latin American republics had no navies, and England and America were still weak from the Revolutionary War, and were building up animosities which were soon to become the War of 1812. While pirates were a constant irritant to all countries, the leading nations could spare neither ships nor men to send on pirate patrol.

In time Gasparilla faced an important problem. His need for a land based headquarters was becoming increasingly more urgent. He needed warehouses for his rich plunder, and stockade for his prisoners awaiting ransom, land for growing fresh vegetables, a place to keep chickens, pigs and cows, and a village where his common pirates could revel in drunken orgies and make love to their women. Above all, he felt a strong personal need for a place to relax among his books, and where he could live like a gentleman between voyages, surrounded by women and slaves to do his bidding.

Such old time pirate strongholds as Tortuga and Goaves were out of the question, for they were too exposed—and known, to offer any degree of safety. The place Gasparilla finally selected was an island at the mouth of Charlotte Harbor on the wild Gulf Coast of Florida. He gave his name to the island, and he called the village his slaves built after the deep water pass at the southern end of the island. Today there is a resort town on the site and the names remain as Gasparilla left them, Boca Grande on Gasparilla Island. The names that Don Jose' gave to the other nearby islands are also retained to this day—Captiva, Sanibel, Cayo Costa and Josefa (also known as Useppa today).

Going back to "The Pirates' Who's Who", an old book published in England and out of print these many years, we read:

"Settling at Charlotte Harbor —" (actually, as we have seen, it was at Boca Grande on Gasparilla Island) — "he built a fort, where he kept his female prisoners, all the males ones being killed. He was fond of fashionable clothes, had very polished manners, and a streak of romance in his nature. When aroused he thought nothing of slicing off a woman's head, or running a sword through a child. He kept his house on Gasparilla Island filled with young and beautiful women that he had captured from ships of every nation. These women's lives were usually short, for he would soon tire of them and give them to his crew or behead them in a fit of temper, and each time a new face appealed to him, one of the less beautiful ones must in some way make room for the new."

On the inner island of Cara Pelau Gasparilla built a village where the most vicious of his crew could carouse to their hearts content, and not bother him with their constant yells and drunken fights. He also found it necessary to move the female captives being held for ransom to a safer place than his camp at Boca Grande. The place he selected was a deserted island a few leagues to the south, and it was soon known as Captiva, (Spanish for female captive) and has become the Captiva Island we know today.

Written history has but little to say about the only woman whom Gasparilla was never able to conquer in body or in spirit, and who defied him until the very instant of her death. Again we read from the pages of "The Pirates' Who's Who":

"In 1801, he took a big Spanish ship forty miles from Boca Grande, killed the crew, took a quantity of gold and twelve young ladies. One of these was a Spanish princess— (actually it seems that she was the youngest daughter of a former Spanish Viceroy of Mexico, by name Josefa de Mayorga)—whom he kept for himself; the eleven Mexican girls he gave to his crew . . . the little Spanish princess would have none of him, and was murdered."

In the hands of Gasparilla the lot of Josefa was, to say the least, a most unhappy one. He is said to have fallen violently in love with the young woman, and to have tried by every means to make her become his willing mistress. He compelled the other women of his household to honor her every wish, and he showered her with jewels, fancy gowns, and even a private apartment of her own.

As the story comes down to us Gasparilla used amazing self restraint in his courtship of Josefa, but the girl was arrogant, spoiled and willful. She recognized him for what he had become; a thief and a cutthroat, and she called him hard names to his face. After a few months of this one sided courtship Jose' Gaspar's patience reached the breaking point. A history book tells us that Gasparilla finally be-

"Black Caesar" the ex-slave, who turned pirate and for a time made Sanibel Island his headquarters.

came insane over the girl's repeated rebuffs, and — "in a fit of temper he drew his sword and neatly beheaded the Princess with one mighty blow."

There may have been a bit of exaggeration in the above quotation, but it seems clear that the poor girl was murdered by Gasparilla's hand, or order, and that the execution took place on Josefa's Island, which is still so named on the official map of Lee County, Florida.

Before and during the War of 1812 the pirates of the Gulf and West Indies had things very much their own way, but after the war had ended the United States Navy began to patrol these waters.. Also added to the pirates' woes was the fact that merchant ships were becoming better armed and manned, and were no longer to be taken without a pitched battle. The game was fast becoming unworthy of the risk.

One by one the lesser pirates sailed away to try their luck in Central or South America. The La Fitte brothers of New Orleans moved to Galveston Island off the Mexican State of Texas, and then into oblivion, and at last only Gasparilla and his wicked crew remained in the Gulf. When the United States and Spain began to negotiate the transfer of the Florida Territory to U.S. sovereignty, Gasparilla read the handwriting on the wall. He began to make plans to leave Boca Grande and move to South America.

News came in 1821 that the United States had formally taken possession of Florida, and that the United States Navy were fitting out a fleet at Norfolk, Virginia, to make war on any pirates remaining in the Gulf or Caribbean. Upon hearing this Gasparilla began breaking up his village at Boca Grande. He was now the age of 65 and well supplied with goods and treasure, and had no desire to come to grips with the United States ships, especially now that a few ships were being powered by steam as well as sail.

The next weeks were busy ones for Gasparilla's men. Caches of gold and silver were dug from their hiding places, the warehouses were emptied of everything of great value, and the Negro slaves and women prisoners were turned loose to shift for themselves.

On the morning that Gasparilla planned to leave the coast of Florida forever, the lookout in the watch tower

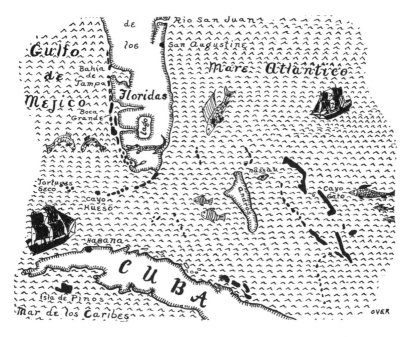

A section of an old map of the early 1700's found between the pages of an old book in a Key West antique shop.

sighted a large ship, apparently becalmed, just a few miles off the mouth of Boca Grande pass. The craft bore the marks of a British merchantman, and appeared to be easy prey for Gasparilla's rough and ready crew.

The thought of taking one more prize before sailing away was too much for the pirates to resist, so Gasparilla's vessel, loaded with ill gotten treasure as she was, swept out of Boca Grande pass on a fast ebb tide, and made for the stranger. Only when they were well within range did

the pirates realize that they had been tricked. The false sides of the stranger fell away to reveal rows of guns, and the American flag broke out at the peak. At almost the same moment the American ship, the *Enterprise*, fired a broadside that caught the pirate craft below the water line.

Moments later shot and chain raked the damaged vessel fore and aft, and left a path of destruction and death.

Realizing that one of his own tricks had been used against him, and with certain defeat staring him in the face, Gasparilla rushed to the bow and screamed a curse at the American ship. Then, feeling his vessel going down under his feet, he flung his sword aside with a fierce oath, twisted a length of anchor chain around his slim waist, shook his fist toward the *Enterprise*, and threw himself into the Gulf.

And so ended the long and ruthless career of Jose' Gaspar, alias Gasparilla. He had been in turn a Spanish officer of high rank, a pirate, a seducer of countless women, a wholesale murderer of human souls, and the last, and perhaps greatest, of all the pirates who operated in the 1800s.

There is little more to tell. Most of Gasparilla's crew were drowned, or captured and hung by the Americans. A few who had been left ashore at Boca Grande to guard such of the treasure which had yet to be loaded, saw the plight of their companions, and made their escape down Pine Island Sound in a yawl. They soon quarreled among themselves and separated. Black Augustus, Gasparilla's chief gunner, remained on Black Island in Estero Bay to end his days, while Juan Gomez remained at Panther Key for a time. Another managed to return to Cuba, but of the rest who escaped from Boca Grande nothing is known. And so ended the life of Jose' Gaspar, who became a pirate to avenge a wrong done to him by those in high places of the Spanish Government.

Juan Gomez —
The Pirate of Panther Key

Time: 1778-1900   *Place*: *Panther Key*

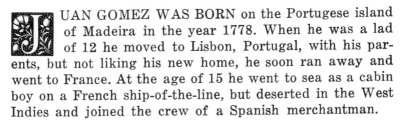UAN GOMEZ WAS BORN on the Portugese island of Madeira in the year 1778. When he was a lad of 12 he moved to Lisbon, Portugal, with his parents, but not liking his new home, he soon ran away and went to France. At the age of 15 he went to sea as a cabin boy on a French ship-of-the-line, but deserted in the West Indies and joined the crew of a Spanish merchantman.

The name of the Spanish vessel was the *Villa Rica*, one of the last of the galleons, and while aboard her he visited many parts of the world: St. Augustine, Vera Cruz, Pensacola, Puerto Rico, Cadiz, Barcelona, and many another port in South America and the Caribbean. He was still aboard the *Villa Rica* in 1801, when she was blown far off course during the late September hurricane and was captured, looted, and burned while forty miles off the Florida Gulf coast, by the pirate, Gasparilla, and his bloody crew.

All the crew of the doomed ship were knifed and dropped over the side save young Juan Gomez, who was only saved by Gasparilla's personal intervention. Also spared—for a time, at least—were eleven young Mexican girl passengers bound for school in Spain, and the young and handsome daughter of a former Mexican Viceroy. The Mexican girls were divided among the pirate crew, but Gasparilla kept the young Mexican girl, Josefa, for himself, only to later behead her in a fit of rage.

Gasparilla took a great liking for young Gomez, and soon made him a full member of the pirate Brotherhood. Some four years later Gasparilla sent Juan Gomez to Spain on a mission of murder. The man whom Gasparilla wished assassinated was his sworn enemy, Manuel de Godoy, the Spanish Prime Minister.

Gomez reached Spain but before he could get to Madrid to carry out his assignment, he was caught in a levy and made to become a member of the Black Dragoons, and was stationed near the French border. He was on sentry duty at this border point when a French army under the personal command of Napoleon Bonaparte marched into Spain. While the horses of Napoleon's carriage were being fed and watered, General Bonaparte patted Juan Gomez on the shoulder, and said the youth would make a fine soldier someday—perhaps even an officer. A short time after this, Juan deserted his post, made his way to Bilboa, and sailed before the mast on a bark bound for Charleston, in the Carolinas.

A year later Juan Gomez was a member of the crew of a slave ship, sailing between Africa and various ports in the West Indies. He was still in the slave trade in 1818 when his ship fell into the hands of one of Gasparilla's captains, and being recognized, his life was spared, and he was taken to meet with Gasparilla at Boca Grande.

Juan Gomez, now about the age of 43, was still at Boca Grande in 1821 when Gasparilla sailed out of Charlotte Harbor to capture what he thought was a merchant vessel. Instead it was one of Admiral Porter's pirate patrol American warships in disguise. From the shore Gomez watched as Gasparilla's vessel took a broadside and began to sink. Realizing the game was up, he and a few other pirates who had been left ashore, climbed into a yawl and escaped down Pine Island Sound.

Juan Gomez hid on Panther Key for a time, but in 1825 he was picked up by a coasting schooner and taken to Havana. He spent the next five years aboard another slave ship, but in 1831 he became involved in a revolt against the Spanish authorities in Cuba, and only escaped capture and death by putting out to sea in a small boat. He was near death from thirst and the tropic sun when a passing ship took him aboard and left him at St. Augustine.

The days of pirates and slave ships were about over, so Gomez remained in North Florida, doing odd jobs and fishing for a living. At the age of 57 he joined General Zachary Taylor's command as a scout, and served in a part of the Seminole War. He was in the battle of Lake Okeechobee on Christmas Day of 1837. He was mustered out about a year later, and spent the next few years at herding cattle in the vicinity of Cedar Keys on the Gulf Coast. In 1855, at the age of 77, he returned to Panther Key and lived in a palmetto shack.

The first white man to meet Juan Gomez after his return to Panther Key was Captain Walter T. Collier, a trader who brought his family to live on Marco Island about 1870. The Captain reported that Gomez seemed to be well supplied with money at the time, and often hinted that he had done considerable blockade running during the Civil War. The ex-pirate was then about 92 years old by his own reckoning, but was still heavy set, with dark eyes and a heavy beard, and able to climb tall coconut palms after milk nuts.

Captain William D. Collier, son of W. T. Collier, operated the schooner *Robert E. Lee,* on trading missions between Tampa, Cedar Keys and Key West and later, about

1890, built a concrete store at Marco (still in use) and started the Marco Lodge about the same time. He knew Juan Gomez from 1872 until the old man's death in July of 1900, and had many a heart-to-heart talk with the old ex-pirate.

Captain Bill Collier told me that Gomez used to disappear in his little sailing sharpie for weeks at a time, but where he went on these trips was always a secret. There was some speculation that he was away digging for treasure. At various times Gomez hinted that he knew the location of some of Gasparilla's loot, and even sold several crude maps to gullible strangers purporting to show just where to dig. However he always explained his absences to Captain Collier by saying that he had been away hunting a wife.

In 1884 Juan Gomez returned from one of his mysterious trips and brought a woman with him. He said they had been married at Tampa, but neither he nor the woman would tell anything of her background. She was, however, a woman of some education, and spoke good English. According to Captain Collier, she was well preserved for her admitted age of 78.

A few more years passed and Captain Bill Collier began to notice that Gomez was buying less and less from the Marco Trading Post. A time came when the old pirate failed to appear at Marco Island for a period of three months. On his next trip to Key West Captain Collier put in at Panther Key to investigate. He found Gomez and the woman to be lean and rather hungry looking. They had been living on coconuts, palm cabbage, coon oysters, fish and clams. There was not an ounce of store bought food left on the island. In spite of Juan's many claims of knowing where treasure was to be found, the couple did not have a dollar left to their name.

On his next trip to Fort Myers, Captain Collier paid a visit to the Commissioners of the recently organized County of Lee, and placed the plight of Gomez and the woman before them. As a result the County reluctantly authorized Captain Bill to supply them with $8.00 worth of food or clothing per month, and send the bill to the County Clerk for payment.

A little later a pair of strangers sailed up to Panther Key and asked Gomez for permission to camp on the beach. One of the men took a great liking for the island, and ended up making Juan Gomez a proposition. He offered to build Gomez a stout dwelling from driftwood and the wreck of a schooner on a nearby reef, and in return Gomez would sign a will leaving the man, Sampson Brown, all of Gomez's squatter's rights to Panther Key. It was quite evident that Sampson Brown, being not more than 50 years old, expected to outlive Gomez who claimed to be about 112 at the time. As it turned out, however, Sampson Brown died eight years before Gomez gave up his last breath of life.

Gradually the news of the old ex-pirate living on a tropical paradise down among the Ten Thousand Islands of Florida's lower Gulf coast, reached the ears of. yachtsmen of the 1880's and '90's. Hardly a year passed without at least three or four sail or steam yachts visiting Panther Key for a talk with the strange character.

For a small handout of food, clothing or money, the old pirate would spin fantastic tales of his days as a buccaneer, or his years in the African slave trade. He would tell, too, of chests heavy with rich plunder, buried beneath the roots of a gumbo-limbo tree, under a slab of native stone, or deep in the side of an Indian mound on one of the inner keys.

He would mumble of casks filled with doubloons, and of kegs of pieces-of-eight minted in Mexico for the King of Spain. At other times he made mention of jewels — rubies, diamonds and emeralds, and of large chunks of solid gold, melted down from finger rings, church ornaments, or earrings knifed from the flesh of female prisoners. For a small fee he would make the markings of a "treasure map" for the gullible to follow.

On a hot July day in the year 1900 Juan Gomez, then a ripe 122 by his own claim, set sail for some off-shore fishing in his tiny catboat. While throwing his castnet over a school of mullet, his shrunken legs became entangled in the draw cord of his net, and he was pitched over the side, head down, in the sea. Several days later some fishermen out of Chokoloskee Island found his drifting boat, with the bloated body still fast to the twisted cord.

Captiva, Once an Isle of Captive Women

Time: 1800 *to* 1821   *Place*: *Captiva Island*

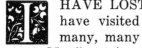HAVE LOST TRACK of the number of times I have visited Sanibel and Captiva Islands in the many, many years I have lived on Florida's Suncoast. My first trips to these storied isles were made in the steamboats *Gladys* and *Dixie*, operated by the Kinzie Brothers, and then in the mailboat, *Santiva*. At other times I visited the islands in a skiff with outboard motor, or in a guide boat, but in recent years I have taken my car over on the ferry several times each season, and have spent many an hour driving along the beach, or traveling the highways and sand trails of these peaceful outer keys.

Only in our times, however, have these delightful green isles, set in the bluegreen waters of a tropic sea, enjoyed the peace and quietude they now enjoy. In those years when these islands, and all the rest of Florida, belonged to the King of Spain, one might have heard the drunken howls of pirates, or the anguished cries of slave or prisoner echoing upon these sandy shores. Long before that one might have heard the war cries of savage Indians as they battled adventurous Spaniards who stepped upon these shores in their quest for gold or the Fountain of Youth.

The pirate Gasparilla, to name but one of that ilk, made use of these and other islands in the chain, and was driven out just about 50,000 days ago, or less than 140 years as time is usually counted. It was in 1821 when Gasparilla, met his death off Boca Grande, just a few miles to the north of Captiva Island. In spite of the passing years much of these islands remain just about as the pirates left them, and herein lies much of their charm for people with a romantic streak.

Sanibel—probably a contraction of Santa Isabel—was once the home of Black Caesar, a pirate of sinister character, and according to some stories, was also the place where the pirate, Gasparilla, brought his stolen goods to sell them to Jean La Fitte for good American gold. La Fitte, in turn, carried off the plunder in his own ships to Barrataria Bay, to be smuggled into New Orleans and sold at bargain prices.

The name of Sanibel's sister island, Captiva, comes from the Spanish word, *cautiva*, which means a female slave or captive. In times past the name was well taken, for on this verdant isle Gasparilla is said to have quartered certain of his valuable female captives for safe keeping until their ransom money could be paid. Of course there is no positive proof, today, that the wives or daughters of wealthy families were detained in a stockade on Captiva Island, for all we have to go on in this regard are the word of mouth stories handed down over almost a century and a half of time. Yet the overall picture seems plausible—even reasonable—in the light of what we do know of pirate methods back in the 1800's. Then, too, how else would you explain the name of Captiva—the captive isle?

Travel by sea in the days of sailing ships, especially for women, was not only rough but fraught with danger. There was no such thing as a passenger ship, and the best to be expected was a small cabin or two. In many a case the passengers were confined to a space in the hold, along with the cargo and perhaps a few large ship's rats for companions. Few traveled for pleasure in the days when pirates scoured the seas, and women went to sea only as pioneers to a new land, or to follow a government worker or soldier to his new post.

Pirates had discovered centuries before that the wife or daughter of a wealthy merchant, or of any high official, who fell into their hands could be turned into a fair sum of gold by means of ransom. This method of capital gain was still popular in Gasparilla's day, and according to the evidence we have he used this form of extortion to the utmost. His ransom demands, along with an assurance that no harm would befall the lady if the money be paid, were handled by his agent in Havana. As soon as the agent reported that the sum demanded had been placed to Gasparilla's credit, the lady in question would be deposited on a beach near some town or village, usually on the Island of Cuba.

It is said that Gasparilla was meticulous in trying to honor his written promise that no harm would befall the lady during the weeks or months of her captivity, and each time his promise was violated by some act of his men, he would fly into a rage and punish the guilty one by sudden death with sword or pistol. It was after some of his men, made courageous by too much drink, had staged a night raid on the prison compound at Boca Grande—and several ladies of quality had been carried off—that Gasparilla ordered a new stockade built on an island some two leagues to the south where women prisoners awaiting the payment of ransom could be kept in safety. A few of Gasparilla's old and trusted men acted as guards, and this island soon became known as La Isla de los Cautivas. The Island of the Captives.

The log stockade that surrounded this camp, as well as the thatched huts where the prisoners lived while awaiting their deliverance, have long gone the way of all organic matter in the tropics. Nothing remains on Captiva today to prove that there once was a woman's prison hidden somewhere on the island. All we have is the word of some of the earliest settlers, who in turn claimed to have heard it from the few of Gasparilla's men who escaped hanging, and lived out their last years on one of the Florida keys.

Just where the camp was on Captiva Island, no one now alive seems to know. That it was located in one of the natural coconut groves seems assured, and that it was well hidden from the Gulf of Mexico is certain. We must also assume that in those distant years the island knew many a heart filled with fear, and with troubled waiting.

On a day not long ago I sprawled lazily on a bed of needles under an Australian pine, and watched a changing pattern of billowy clouds scudding over Captiva Island. My eyes closed and slowly a picture came. It was a picture of many women, some young, some matronly, some with the regal air of nobility. Each went about some task; tending a cooking fire, cleaning fish for the evening meal, husking coconuts for their milk, stirring a bubbling kettle over a driftwood fire. Such tasks were new to most, for in the homes they had left there had been servants or slaves for such menial tasks. Now they looked forward to keeping busy with their hands as a means of forgetting their troubles—at least for the moment.

The blast of an auto horn on the cement bridge between Captiva and Sanibel brought me back to reality. I looked at my watch. I had less than an hour to travel the length of Sanibel, and get the Cadillac on the last afternoon ferry bound for the mainland at Punta Rassa. As always I longed to remain on the sister islands of Sanibel and Captiva, but business would not permit a longer stay. As I rolled the car onto the ferry I knew one thing for sure; I would be back.

*   *   *   *

And back I have gone many a time since the new causeway and bridges to these romantic islands were opened to the public in 1963. No longer does one have to depend or wait for the ferry boats of former years. A new age has dawned for Sanibel and Captiva.

The Pirate
and the Golden Haired Virgin

Time: 1794 *to* 1823   *Place*: *Pavilion Key*

HIS IS THE TRUE STORY of Charles Gibbs, pirate, whose life span of twenty-nine years between birth and hanging, was still of sufficient length to allow him to become one of the most villianous freebooters of his time. He was born on a farm near Providence, Rhode Island, in the year 1794. While still a boy in his lower 'teens he ran away to sea, and served his apprenticeship aboard the United States sloop-of-war, *Harriet*. In the War of 1812 he saw action against H.M.S. *Peacock*, and afterwards served on board the *Chesapeake* during her famed battle with the *Shannon*. He was taken prisoner and carried to England.

In due time Charles Gibbs was released from Dartmoor Prison, where he had been confined as a prisoner of war, and opened up a grog shop on Ann Street, called the "Tin Pot." It soon became the hangout of drunks, perverts, pickpockets and all the "abandoned women" of the neighborhood. In a short time—all his profits having been used up in swilling his own merchandise—he was compelled to go to sea again. On the waterfront he met Johnathan Bell, captain and owner of a Columbian privateer, and soon had a berth aboard the *Maria* in the capacity of able seaman.

The *Maria* spent the next two months in cruising around Cuba, and in the Gulf of Mexico, but the crew became dissatisfied in consequence of the non-payment of prize monies due them, and a mutiny arose. The crew, under Gibbs' leadership, took possession of the privateer, and landed Captain Bell and the mate on an island beach near Pensacola, Florida. A meeting was next held, during which some of the mutineers voiced a desire to continue operations under the Columbian flag, while ohers insisted on flying the Black Flag. The latter group, noisily led by Gibbs, had their way in the end, and a black flag was hoisted as a declaration of war against any and all nations.

A Spanish member of the crew named Paco del Gordo (Fat Frank) suggested that an arrangement could be made with a certain shifty merchant in Havana, who would receive and sell all manner of stolen goods, and divide the resulting profits on an even basis. He had learned of this man while he had been a member of a gang of pirates under the leadership of the infamous Jose' Gaspar, or Gasparilla. The suggestion was favorably received and Gibbs steered the *Maria* to within a few miles of Morro Castle at the mouth of Havana harbor, and Paco del Gordo was put ashore to make arrangements with the dishonest merchant.

The *Maria* now set out on a course of rape and murder. Some additional cutthroats had been recruited from the waterfront dives of Havana, and the pirates taking orders from Gibbs now numbered about fifty. The first vessel to come afoul of their guns was the *Indispensable*, an English ship, bound for Havana, which was easily taken and sailed to the vicinity of Cape San Antonio at the western tip of Cuba. The crew of the *Indispensable*, were brutally murdered to the last man, and their bloodied bodies were dropped to the waiting sharks.

Such treatment became the pattern for all future prisoners. The unhappy prisoner who begged for mercy, in the hope that something like humanity might be found in the heart of even the worst of men, shared the same fate as those who resolved to sell their lives at the highest possible price. A French brig with a valuable cargo of wine and silk was taken shortly after, with the entire crew being butchered and the ship burned.

The sanguinary scenes through which Gibbs had led his men had now effectively wrought their desperation to fever pitch, and no longer did he have to urge any man of his crew to begin the bloody slaughter. He had called for a show of hands, and the ship's company—without a single objector—had voted to spare no lives, and to burn all ships falling into their hands.

Gibbs now directed the *Maria* towards the Dry Tortugas, where they soon captured a brig, believed to have been the *William* of New York, bound for Vera Cruz, Mexico, with a cargo of furniture. The crew of the *William* were knifed and tossed into the sea, while a prize crew sailed the ship to Cape Antonio, so that the cargo could be sent to their agent in Havana. Sometime during this cruise the pirate craft was chased for a whole day by a United States ship-of-war, supposed to have been the *John Adams*, but Gibbs managed to escape into Florida Bay with the coming of night.

In the early summer of 1817 they captured the *Earl of Moira*, an English vessel from the London Pool, with a cargo of bolt goods and findings. The crew were promptly murdered, the goods sent on to Havana, and the ship fired. In return they received a sizeable cash payment from the Havana agent, and the proceeds of their inhuman crimes were divided into shares, according to their signed articles of agreement.

During a cruise made in the latter part of 1817, and the beginning of 1818, a Dutch bark from Curacao was cap-

Women prisoners go about their chores at the stockade on Captiva Island while awaiting the arrival of their ransom money.

tured, with a choice cargo of West Indian goods and produce, and a quantity of silver plate. The passengers and crew, to the number of thirty souls were all destroyed, with the single exception of a beautiful virgin of seventeen. This Dutch girl was the youngest daughter of a wealthy island planter, and her name was Kaaren Van Bokkelen. She was a buxom, blue-eyed beauty with golden curls and blushing cheeks, and when it came her time to meet the murderer's thrust, she ran to Gibbs, fell on her knees, and implored the young man to spare her life.

Moved more by sudden lust than by any compassion, Gibbs hauled the quaking girl to her feet and held her in a tight embrace. She hid her face against his shoulder while the pirate crew went on with the murder of the Dutch sailors, and as the butchery continued Gibbs made so bold as to bargain with the hysterical girl for her very life. Even though she understood few of the coarse English words he uttered, she was old enough to grasp his meaning and intent. After casting an agonized glance at the bestial faces of the blood smeared pirates, any one of whom would gladly have raped and then murdered her, the helpless, fear-choked lass could do little else but nod her head in submission.

Charles Gibbs, in spite of the wicked mutterings of his crew, insisted on carrying the unlucky girl to their rest camp on an island below Cape Romano on the Gulf coast of Florida. There, partly with his own hands, Gibbs built a pavilion of logs, with a roof of palm frond thatching, and kept Kaaren a prisoner for her own safety. The pirates, except Gibbs, considered the girl an evil influence, and a positive danger. Her evidence in any court of law could hang every one of them, and they had sworn an oath to leave no living witness to their many crimes. Within a week Gibbs shot and killed one of his gunners who had managed to lay a hand on the girl, with a view of beating her head in with a club. Finally, facing open mutiny, Gibbs was compelled to submit the girl's unhappy fate to a council of war. It was

quickly decided by a vote that the preservation of harmony
—even their very lives in case of capture—made her death
necessary.

When the time came Gibbs could not quite bring himself to spilling the hapless girl's blood with pistol ball,
sword or knife. Instead he ordered the cook to mix a deadly
potion with her food. This was done, and the poor, dispirit-
ed girl suffered a frightful retching and horrible abdomin-
able pains before she died.

A short time later the United States schooner *Porpoise*
of the West Indies squadron, out on pirate patrol, with
Lieutenant James Ramage in command, visited the island
where the pretty Dutch girl had been killed, and found her
unmarked grave. They also discovered the log pavilion
where the girl had been imprisoned, and since the island
had been unnamed up to that time, Lieutenant Ramage pen-
ciled in the name, Pavilion Key, on his charts. It is so known
to this day.

Shortly after this the *Maria* was wrecked on the shore
near Cape Antonio, and was so badly damaged it became
necessary to destroy her on the beach. Gibbs' agent in Havana, who acted as a "fence" for several other pirate bands
in the Caribbean and Gulf, promised to procure another
vessel at a bargain price, and no questions to be asked.
From the pirate, Gasparilla, the agent secured a well found
brigantine recently captured off the coast of Honduras. It
was hidden in the back waters of Charlotte Harbor, but
was soon renamed the *Picciana*, and delivered to the strand-
ed Gibbs and his crew at Cape Antonio.

In this vessel they cruised with fair success for almost
four years. Among the ships taken and destroyed with all
hands were the *Belvidere*, a Dutch brig named the *Dido*,
the British bark *Larch*, and many more whose names are
lost to us. They had a narrow escape at one time from the
English man-o-war *Coronation*. In the early part of October, 1821, they captured a Charleston packet, took her to
Cape Antonio, and were busy lowering her cargo to a crude

dock, when the United States ship, *Enterprise*, Captain Kearney commanding, hove in sight. The warship dared not close in for the kill because of her draft, but sent off her small boats to attack the pirate brigantine and her prize.

A serious engagement followed. The pirates defended themselves for a time behind a four gun battery set up on a low sand dune near the beach. After several hours of bombardment from the *Enterprise*, as well as steady small arms fire from the marines, the United States sailors charged ashore with bayonet, sword and cutlass. The pirates, after suffering considerable loss of numbers, were finally forced to abandon their vessel and booty, and fled to the jungled hills.

At Gibbs' order the pirates left a pot of hot, poisoned coffee over the fire in their cook shack, in the hope that the Americans would be fools enough to drink it down. This statement was confirmed by Captain Kearney of the *Enter-prise*, who stated in his report that the filth of the cooking utensils and camp was more than his men could stomach.

Gibbs escaped to Havana and collected the sum of $30,-000 American dollars from the dishonest merchant. He was next seen briefly on the streets of New York, and confided to a boyhood friend that he intended to retire on his ill gotten gains and live the life of a country squire. Evidently a life of ease was tiring to one so young—he was about the age of twenty-eight—for within a month or two he booked passage on a square rigger bound for Liverpool.

Gibbs had no sooner arrived at the famous port on the River Mersey than he began a round of fleshpots and dives along the waterfront. In one of these Liverpool public houses he met an Irish lass with flaming hair, a honeyed tongue, and freckles across the bridge of her saucy tipped up nose. The rest was an old story; repeated many, many times before and since. The girl, Bridget, made free use of her wiles and charms, and one morning Charles Gibbs awoke to find himself alone in his tumbled bed, and not even a single shilling left to his name.

As a result Gibbs signed on before the mast on a British brigantine bound for New Orleans, but because of harsh treatment he jumped ship as soon as a line was looped over a bollard near the foot of Canal Street. This was in November of 1822, and he immediately found a berth as a seaman aboard the brig *Vineyard*, bound for Philadelphia with a cargo of cotton, molasses and "54,000 dollars in specie."

William Thornby was the master of the *Vineyard*; the mate was a sour faced oldster named William Roberts. The crew consisted of six men and a boy; Charles Gibbs, John Brownrigg, Robert Dawes, Henry Atwell, James Talbott, Arthur Church and Thomas Wansley, a young Negro from the State of Delaware who acted as cook.

Wansley, the Negro cook, had helped the Captain secrete the specie, mostly in gold and silver coins, in the bottom of the lazaret underneath some old sails, while they were alone aboard ship, and had sworn to keep the master's secret. The Vineyard had no more than reached the vicinity of the Dry Tortugas near Key West, than he made it known to the crew about the fortune hidden aboard. This information aroused the cupidity of the crew, especially Gibbs, and he began a discussion as to how the money might fall into their hands. Many meetings were held on the subject, and while these conversations were in progress in the forecastle, Robert Dawes, who was a mere boy, was sent aft to converse with the officers, in order to divert their attention from what was going on.

Brownrigg alone protested against any form of mutiny or piracy, but Gibbs was the master mind, and in the end his will prevailed. It was finally resolved by the majority that as the master and mate were old men, it was time they should die and make room for the rising generation. Then, too, Gibbs pointed out, the mate, Mr. Roberts was of such a peevish disposition that he deserved death. Gibbs made careful plans, and by promises and threats, forced his will on his shipmates.

The murder of the master and mate were set for the night of November 23rd., 1822. Gibbs and Wansley, the Negro cook, were to do away with Captain Thornby, while Atwell and Church were to look after the mate. The vessel was off Cape Hatteras when the hour for the murders arrived. The master was standing on the quarter deck, Dawes had the helm, and Brownrigg was aloft in the crow's nest. Dawes called Wansley aft to trim the light in the binnacle. The Negro moved as if to obey, but coming up behind Mr. Thornby, struck him on the back of the neck with the pump brake, so that he fell forward, crying "murder — murder!" Wansley repeated the blows until the master was dead, and then, with the assistance of Gibbs, threw the body over the side.

While this black deed was being done, the mate, aroused by the noise, came up the companion ladder from his quarters below. Atwell and Church were waiting for him on deck, and struck him down with a club, but failed to kill him. Gibbs followed to complete the work, but not being able to locate the mate in the black of the night, ran to the helm for the binnacle light. It was then discovered that the mate had dropped down the ladder, but going below Gibbs was unable, in the close quarters, to overcome the mate, even with the help of Atwell. Finally with the assistance of Church, the wounded man was hauled on deck where he was savagely beaten and thrown overboard. He was still conscious and swam after the vessel for a minute or two crying for help, before the waves covered him. All these attacks were witnessed by the boy, Dawes, who had a passive, if not an active part in them.

The pirate crew were now in possession of the vessel, and Wansley busied himself with mopping up the blood spilled on deck, declaring with an oath, that though he had heard it said that the blood stains of a murdered person could not be effaced, he knew this to be a lie for he had spilled human blood several times before. Then, after a round of drinks, the conspirators brought up the money from the lazaret. It was distributed in equal parts to all on board.

Gibbs now made himself the new master of the *Vineyard*. He steered a northeasterly course until they were off Long Island some ten or fifteen miles from South Hampton Light. Here they resolved to take to the small boats even though the wind was making a near gale. Atwell scuttled the brig and got into the jolly boat with Church and Talbot, while Gibbs, Wansley, Dawes and Brownrigg put off in the long boat. The jolly boat swamped on a bar two miles from shore, and all on board were drowned. The long boat was in equal danger, and was only saved at the last minute by throwing several bags, heavy with gold and silver pieces, into the sea.

The sole survivors of the *Vineyard*, Gibbs, Wansley, Dawes and Brownrigg, made the beach at Pelican Island, and at once buried what money still remained in their possession. They found a native who told them where they were, and who agreed to ferry them to Great Barn Island. Here they went to the home of a Mr. Johnson, and rented a horse and wagon to carry them further toward the mainland.

It was at this point that Brownrigg, never in favor of the killing of the master and mate, refused to further accompany his companions. To Mr. Johnson he muttered that Gibbs and Wansley were murderers, and had scuttled the *Vineyard*. On learning of this Mr. Johnson sent a messenger to the local magistrate, and Gibbs and Dawes were soon apprehended. Wansley escaped in the woods, but he was followed and captured within hours.

The guilt of Gibbs and Wansley was full and conclusive. They made full confessions of their crimes to two officers, Meritt and Stevenson, who had custody of them on the trip from Flatbush to New York. What persuasion was used in obtaining the confessions, if any, is not known. Wansley told the entire story, occasionally prompted by Gibbs on the more minor details, and both admitted that Brownrigg was innocent of any active participation in their crimes, other than reluctantly accepting a share of the loot. Their confession was not, however, so favorable to the boy, Robert Dawes. Realizing his plight the boy quickly agreed to become a State's witness and testify against the murderous pair.

Gibbs was soon arraigned for the murder of the mate, William Roberts, and Wansley for that of the captain, William Thornby. They were soon tried, found guilty, and the District Attorney moved for immediate judgment on the jury's verdict.

There was nothing peculiar in their deportment during the trial. The iron visage of Gibbs was occasionally darkened during the trial by a transient emotion, especially when the boy, Dawes, and John Brownrigg, gave the most damning testimony, but it was evident that he held no hope of escaping the gallows. For the most part Gibbs sat with his hands between his knees, and surveyed the court scene from beneath lowered brows. Wansley was more agitated, and trembled violently when he arose to hear the verdict of the grim faced jurymen.

The verdict was "Guilty as charged," of course, and the judge made haste to pass sentence. He ordered that each should be placed in the custody of the marshall of the Southern District of New York, and should be "hanged by the neck until dead." The execution was to be carried out on the twenty-second of April, 1823, "between the hours of ten and four o'colck, the hours being those of daylight." The executions took place at high noon. Both Gibbs and the Negro, Wansley, arrived at the gallows accompanied by the marshall, his aids, and some twenty or thirty United States Marines. Two clergymen attended them to the fatal spot, where everything being in readiness and the ropes adjusted about their necks, the Mercy of God was fervently addressed in their behalf. Gibbs remained silent, but Wansley prayed loudly and joined in singing a hymn. The traps were sprung, and silence fell over the gallows-yard as all witnesses watched the convulsive death throes of the doomed men.

The boy, Dawes, was not prosecuted, having been promised leniency for becoming a valuable State's witness. His testimony, and that of Brownrigg, was enough to send the unholy pair to their just rewards. As far as is known the boy, Dawes, was never in trouble again.

Honeymooners of Estero Island

Time: 1720   *Place*: *Fort Myers Beach*

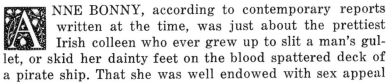

ANNE BONNY, according to contemporary reports written at the time, was just about the prettiest Irish colleen who ever grew up to slit a man's gullet, or skid her dainty feet on the blood spattered deck of a pirate ship. That she was well endowed with sex appeal we must assume, for how else could she have captured the love of a bold and dashing pirate, such as Captain Rackam —better known as "Calico Jack"—when most of the sweet young things of Charleston, Carolina, were not only willing to be crushed in his arms, but positively eager? But wait: we are getting ahead of our story.

Anne was born in Cork, Ireland, and her father was an Attorney-at-Law, and her mother was a lady's maid to the attorney's lawful wife. The scandal was made even worse when the attorney ignored his wife's protests, and kept Anne and the child's mother as members of his household. As a result he lost a once flourishing legal practice, and some years later he up and departed for the Colony of Carolina, and took Anne with him.

In his new surrounding he was favored by fortune, and

soon owned a rich plantation, where Anne kept house for him. Anne grew up to be a handsome woman, but had a "fierce and courageous temper," which more than once led her into scrapes. Once when in "a sad fit of temper," she slew her English serving-maid with a case knife.

Thinking to curb the girl's wild tendencies, her father began to hunt for a suitable husband for Anne. This should have proved easy to accomplish, for aside from her good looks and figure, the girl was destined to inherit her father's sizeable fortune upon his death. However, Anne would have none of the young gentlemen her father approved of, and instead fell in love with, and married, a common sailor of little merit. The young couple thought that when he found the deed done, the father would become reconciled to it. But on the contrary the attorney turned the girl out of his house, and promised never to leave her a shilling.

The young sailor, finding his bride not worth a farthing, soon did what many other sailors have done before and since; he slipped away to sea and never came back. Anne was surprisingly philosophical about the loss of her husband, and was soon visiting Captain Rackam in his cabin aboard his pirate ship. At the time Captain Rackam, better known as Calico Jack because of the shirts he wore, was in good standing with the Governor of Carolina, and the Charleston merchants w e l c o m e d the stolen goods he brought to the city and sold so cheaply.

Now Calico Jack's methods of courting a girl or taking a ship were quite similar — no time wasted, straight up alongside, every gun brought into play, grappling irons away, and the prize seized. Anne was swept off her feet by her picturesque and impetuous lover, and consented to go to sea with him, but disguised herself in sailor's clothes, and cut off her tresses before going aboard.

The cruise, which they considered to be their honeymoon, almost ended in disaster. Their first trouble came

The pirate, Charles Gibbs and the Dutch Girl on Pavilion Key in 1818.

when a Spanish bark they attacked in the waters between Key West and Cuba, made a lucky hit at the base of their mainmast, and brought most of their top-hamper down on their heads. Before this damage could be cleared away a vicious storm struck and drove them up into the Gulf of Mexico. The ship was a shambles above deck, and a new mast had to be found and stepped before the cruise could proceed.

In the edition of Johnson's "History of Highwaymen and Pyrates" published in 1818 by DuPlau of London, there appeared this passage:

" . . . *and so they saw a place of deep water between two islands and made such haste as they could to enter. They discovered there on one island a priest of the Roman Church who was ministering to the savages thereabouts. This priest was by name Father Amadeo, and he made the pyrates welcome as best he might.*

"*The island where they did visit to do away with damage of shot and storm was called Estero, and up a small river of the same name, there were many tall trees suitable after much labour to be carved into a mast and spars. While the ship's carpenter and crew did labour mightily to refit the vessel, Calico Jack and the woman, Anne Bonny, did make merry for many days on the island where they had a dwelling made of sticks and palms.*"

It would seem from a study of the above excerpt that the bold Captain Rackam, and the beauteous lady pirate, were the first white couple to ever honeymoon on the island now known by popular usage as Fort Myers Beach.

In good time Calico Jack put back to sea and resumed his search of victims. Less than a year later the doughty Anne, by now well gone with child, was put ashore in Cuba, and left with a family who were under deep obligation to Calico Jack. A few months after she was delivered Anne was back aboard the pirate ship, and took a hand in several pitched battles. According to history she was "as active as any of her male shipmates with cutlass and marlinspike, always one of the leaders in boarding a prize."

At last there came a day of retribution. While cruising off Jamaica in October of 1720, the pirates were surprised

Anne Bonny and Calico Jack in Estero Bay.

by the sudden appearance of an armed ship sent out by the Governor for the express purpose of capturing Rackam and his crew. A fight followed, in which the pirates behaved in a cowardly manner, and all were driven below decks save Anne Bonny and another woman pirate, Mary Reed, who both fought valiantly until taken prisoners, all the while flaunting their male companions for their sudden cowardice.

The pirate crew were taken to Jamaica and tried for piracy at St. Jago de la Vega, and were convicted on November 28th, 1720. Anne pleaded to have her execution postponed because "of her present condition of health." She was again pregnant, and British law did not countenance the taking of two lives where only one life could be proved guilty.

The records of the Jamaica Government do not show that Anne Bonny was ever hanged for her crimes, but just what her ultimate fate was is not known. On the day that her lover, Rackam, was hanged he obtained, by special favor, permission to see Anne for the last time. However he received little in the way of comfort from the interview, for all he got in the way of sympathy from his former light-o-love were these words—that "she was sorry to see him about to hang from a rope, but if he had fought like a Man, he need not go to be hanged like a Dog."

And so on this sad note we must conclude our tale of a "pirate bold" and an Irish lass from County Cork, who once lived to love on the silver sands of Estero Island—or, if you prefer, we can give it the modern name of Fort Myers Beach.

The Black Pirate of Sanibel Island

Time: 1767 *to* 1818   *Place: Islands of Haiti & Sanibel*

ENRI CAESAR, or Black Caesar as he is better known today, was born into slavery on the Island of Hispaniola, in the French colony of Saint Dominique (now the Republic of Haiti) in the year 1767. His mother was an African slave owned by the wealthy Arnaut family, proprietors of lush valley lands surrounding the village of Verrettes. Due to the loose morals of colonial plantation life in those days, his father will always remain unknown. Young Henri grew rapidly, and at the age of eight was sent to live in the masters' house, where he served as one of the houseboys.

Here he ran errands, worked in the kitchens, carried bathwater for the French ladies, tugged at their corset strings, and during the long and leisurely meals of the master's family, he pulled steadily on a rope that operated the large, cloth covered frame of the punkah, so that a gentle breeze would be felt in the long dining hall. While the boy labored behind the screen, he observed the ways of his French masters, and listened to their private conversations. There was much he would never understand, but he did learn things which were to prove of use in his later years.

The first great change in Henri's life came as he neared his sixteenth year. He was large for his age now—six feet and still growing—and while his muscular growth had not kept pace, he had broad shoulders and a barrel-like chest. His fall from grace was caused by his clumsy hands and huge feet, as well as by his visage, which was slowly growing mean—almost fierce. His awkward hands had dropped delicate porcelains, his feet had tripped over carpets, and his face had brought howls of fear from white children who had come to visit from neighboring plantations, and from Port-au-Prince. A day came when Master Arnaut ordered Henri out of the house, and sent him to labor in the saw-yard.

Henri's new task was the hardest kind of work, and he soon developed a strength to match his bulk; great rippling muscles that pulled and strained as he toiled almost naked under the pitiless Caribbean sun. Balanced on a high-placed mahogany log, he stroked his end of a gleaming two-man saw, and helped shower his saw-mate below with a steady rain of reddish dust. From sun-up to sun-down, six days a week, the slaves of the saw-yard moved in time to a chanted rhythm, separating the huge imported Honduran logs into planks, ready for shipment to Europe. There was always a French overseer waiting, whip in hand, ready to draw blood from the back of any slave who dared pause without permission.

Henri had been happy with his station in life while living at the Master's house. There his tasks had been easy, and his belly had become used to accommodating all the scraps of fancy foods left at the family table. Now everything was different. Twelve hours a day he was forced to strain and sweat in the saw-yard, and for food he had only the simple fare coming from the big cooking pots of the slave quarters; boiled plantains, baked casava roots, rice, and sometimes the lean meat of a wild boar. Most nights found him too tired of body to accept the bold invitation of the young slave women who came to feel the bulging muscles of his arms, or marvel at the smoothness of his massive chest.

Slowly, day by day, the seeds of hate began to sprout in Henri's sluggish brain. Each day of labor, and each cut of the saw-master's whip, added smouldering embers to the banked fires within his skull. His gathering hatred was directed against the white man who shouted orders, and who swung the rawhide whip; it was not against the system whereby one man enslaved another. Had he always labored in the saw-yard, or had he remained at the big house, Henri would have been content with his lot; the thing he resented was the sudden change in his fortunes.

At night Henri heard the rumblings of unrest in the slave compound, and as time went on the murmurs of revolt spread from lip to lip, and along jungle trails from one plantation to the next. There would come a day, the *Papa Loi*, or Voodoo priest, promised, when the black men would toss off their yoke and drive the white men into the sea. These things Henri heard—even thought well of—but he did little to further the cause of revolution.

Henri Caesar was twenty-eight and still toiling in the saw-yard, when the fires of revolt were suddenly ignited. Like a wind driven flame the halocaust spread through the Colony, leaving the land heavy with the smoke of burning mansions, and the sounds of riot, rapine and murder. Under the military genius of a former slave, Toussaint l'Ouverture, and his equally black successor, Dessalines, the slaves eventually defeated a large army sent from France, and commanded by the brother-in-law of the great Napoleon.

Henri did nothing to advance the cause of his people until the Arnaut slaves fired all the outbuildings, and laid siege to the big house. Then, while the howling mob raped and butchered the Arnaut family—even to the youngest child—Henri dragged Jean Folquet, the white overseer of the saw-yard from beneath his bed. With the help of several of his saw-mates they bound the doomed Frenchman between two thick planks, like the meat filling of a giant sandwich. By the light of the burning piles of lumber Henri and his saw-mate began to chant as they stroked the saw through the mahogany planks. They entered the blade near Jean Folquet's feet, sawed between his ankles, between his knees, between his thighs, and then into the poor man's bowels. The unfortunate fellow's screams ended only when the coarse steel teeth bit close to his heart.

For the next nine years Henri Caesar roamed the jungle trails with a band of black followers, engaging in murder, pillage and rape. They fought the French troops by preparing ambushes along mountain trails, or by knifing sentries at their lonely outposts. By the time France gave up the fight and ordered her remaining soldiers home, the land was too poor to support the countless, shiftless bands of ex-slaves, and many were starving on an island capable of producing an overabundance. As a last resort Henri led his little band into a new field of endeavor.

A day in 1805 found Henri Caesar at Port de Paix on the north coast of the island. Just before sunset he spied a becalmed Spanish merchantman standing out several leagues from shore. When night fell he stole a small fishing wherry and, with his gang, paddled out to the ship. Their surprise attack was successful, and all but the captain and three of the crew were immediately murdered. It was a new experience for Henri, and he decided at that moment to go into the pirating business, and needed his prisoners to teach him how to handle the vessel. He treated the Spaniards well enough for several months. Then, having decided he had learned enough to become his own sailing master, he stabbed the prisoners one by one, and dropped them into the sea.

Henri Caesar—or Caesar le Grand, as he liked to call himself—was never as great a pirate as many others of his time, but did have the distinction of being the most ruthless of the lot. No white man or woman ever fell into his hands, and escaped to tell about it. At sea he attacked only the weak and defenseless; ashore he raided and plundered only small, isolated villages or fish camps, and it is said he sped on the wind from any well gunned ship, or from anyone offering anything like an equal battle.

Up to the War of 1812 Caesar le Grand stuck close to the Bahama Channel, and along the key fringed Cuban coast, but during the war he took greater chances, and several times visited the shores of America. After the close of hositlities British ships-of-war returned to the Caribbean area, and after several narrow escapes, Henri headed into the Gulf of Mexico, looking for a safer base of operations.

It has been told that Captain Caesar arranged a meeting with the famous pirate, Gasparilla, and asked to be allowed to join the Brotherhood and sail under Gasparilla's flag. This meeting probably took place at some neutral ground—possibly the Dry Tortugas—for Gasparilla would never allow other pirates to use his anchorage at Charlotte Harbor. As it comes down to us it would seen that Gasparilla did not take Caesar and his crew into the Brotherhood, for he had little personal liking for the black ex-slave who kept thumping his chest and saying, "I am Caesar the Great."

Instead Gasparilla is said to have suggested that Black Caesar establish a camp of his own on Sanibel Island, near the mouth of San Carlos Bay. The Pass at Boca Grande was well fortified with shore batteries, and Gasparilla feared no attack from that direction, but he had long been worried by the open and unguarded reaches of Pine Island Sound to the south. With Black Caesar holding forth on Sanibel Island, no enemy could sail up the Sound without an alarm being given.

As a result of the conference Black Caesar built a village of rough palm thatched huts on the bay side of Sanibel, somewhere near the former ferry landing. When not at sea Black Caesar and his mongrel crew—there were some Cubans among his men—lived ashore with a motley group of camp followers and mangy dogs. As far is now known today, no male prisoners were ever brought to the island, and no white woman ever long survived under the horrible conditions there prevailing.

Captain Caesar is supposed to have captured a large amount of treasure, and some of it might well have been hidden on Sanibel. If such were the case there are no publicly known treasure maps, nor any substantiated story of anyone finding anything of more than nominal value. Several well equipped treasure hunters are known to have gone over parts of the island in recent years, but if they discovered a cache for their trouble, they were not the kind to brag about it.

Black Caesar is said to have had a bitter argument with Gasparilla about 1817 or 1818. According to the story later told by Juan Gomez—one of Gasparilla's men—the trouble came over a raid several of Caesar's drunken men made on Gasparilla's prison stockade on Captiva Island. In this sneak attack two women being held for ransom were stolen, and one of Gasparilla's trusted guards was killed, and another knifed. Flying into a rage, Gasparilla ordered Caesar to leave the Florida coast—at once. Being far weaker in both men and guns Black Caesar had no choice but to comply. Mouthing unearthly threats, he loaded his men and camp followers aboard ship, set fire to his village, and sailed towards the south. Whatever became of the ex-slave who liked to call himself Caesar le Grand, is unknown to this very day.

Treasure at Key Largo

Time: 1909   Place: Key Largo

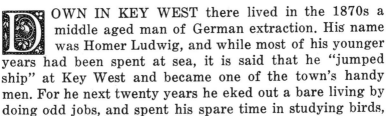OWN IN KEY WEST there lived in the 1870s a middle aged man of German extraction. His name was Homer Ludwig, and while most of his younger years had been spent at sea, it is said that he "jumped ship" at Key West and became one of the town's handy men. For he next twenty years he eked out a bare living by doing odd jobs, and spent his spare time in studying birds, fish, and the history of the Island City.

To all who would, or wanted to listen, he would tell in his deep German accent, the history of Key West. He would explain how the warlike Seminole Indians entered Florida from the north, and usurped the lands of the more peaceful Indians who called themselves the Caloosas. He would tell how the Seminoles drove the Caloosas before them, killing those who resisted, until finally the remnants of the unhappy tribe reached the end of the mainland, and were forced to hop from island to island. At last all that remained of the Caloosas reached the island now known as Key West, and were there forced to make their final stand. In a battle that lasted for days the savage Seminoles

killed the Caloosas to the last man, and left their bones to
bleach under the tropic sun.

"Und ven der first white peoples come—the Spaniards,"
he would explain, "dey found der whole island covered
mit bones. So, dey call der island Cayo Hueso, which means
Bone Key. Den der English come und took der island, und
dey can't say Cayo Hueso so good, so dey call der place
Key West."

One day in the early 1890s Homer bought a small and
decrepit sail boat, and began to spend his spare time in
patching it up. To those who took the trouble to ask why
he wanted a boat, he would explain that he intended to
go treasure hunting. He claimed to have learned the location of a money chest removed from a vessel wrecked on
a reef, but none took him seriously. His friends at Key
West thought the old man was getting childish. He would
talk at length about how the captain of the doomed ship
had carried the money ashore, and buried it in the sand
for safe keeping, intending to return with another vessel
and reclaim the treasure.

"But der captain was killed und no come back," Homer
was willing to explain, "I know almost where iss—der
captain he put map of der island in a book—I got it here,"
then he would point to his head. "What I do now iss find
der right island."

Several weeks later Homer set sail in his little catboat
and was never seen at Key West again. However reports
concerning the old man came back from time to time. A
fisherman had seen the old fellow on the beach of Big Pine
Key, and a little later a yacht had sighted a man of Homer's description at Matecumbe Key. A year later a couple
of Key Westers met Homer on the beach at Key Largo.
The old man had built himself a shack of driftwood and
palm fronds, and he seemed fit and hard as nails. He was
about seventy-five at the time, but they said he was as spry
as an ordinary man of fifty.

Women prisoners aboard a pirate ship in the 1800's
(*After a famous painting by Montania*)

The rest of this story was told to me years later by an ex-fishing guide by the name of Med Kellum. Med had been a professional guide on the Florida Keys until he married a wealthy woman and took life easy. When I knew him he was driving a Cadillac and lived in a sort of mansion he and his wealthy wife had built at Whiskey Creek, on Mc-Gregor Boulevard near Fort Myers. That was in the early 1920s.

"I knew the Dutchman, Homer Ludwig, when he lived on Key Largo over on the East Coast," Med told me. "I used to see him from time to time, from about 1893 until 1909. He was a funny chap, always afraid someone was following him—and they often were. The story got around that Homer had found some loot of some kind, and some of the squatters took to hounding the old man, trying to see where he got his money.

"You wouldn't have thought Homer had a cent to his name, considering the kind of shack he lived in, and the rags he wore, but he always had money when I knew him. Not a lot of money at any one time, you understand, but he could always scrape up forty or fifty dollars anytime he needed it. What made folks curious was that Homer never did any work, and he never got anything in the mail. One week he might be down to maybe five dollars, and a week or so later he might have as much as a hundred.

"Old Homer's shack was ransacked at least a dozen times while he was away in his boat, but the boys who did it never found anything worth carrying away. They even dug up under the shack a couple of times, but there wasn't a thing there but common dirt.

"Another funny thing about Homer was that, with all the fish there was in Florida Bay and out in the Gulf Stream, the old fellow lived mostly on canned sardines and soda crackers. Can you imagine that? Every time he sailed up to what was then the little town of Miami, he'd come back with a couple cases of imported sardines and a stack of cracker boxes. Why out in back of his shack there was a pile of old sardine tins as high as your head, and enough flies to make a dark cloud. I know—I saw 'em myself.

"The old man had been living there on Key Largo maybe five or six years before I found out where he was getting his money." Med Kellum resumed after a moment. "Then a fellow who ran a general store in Miami told me that Homer was selling old gold and silver coins, a few at a time, to a coin dealer on Flagler Street. He'd sell his old money for fifty, or maybe a hundred dollars, then go and buy a few things—like a pair of overalls, or a shirt, and load up with sardines and crackers, with maybe a few cans of peaches, and sail back to Largo.

"When this news got out is when the islanders began to try and learn where Homer was getting the treasure. They tried following him after he went into the brush, but the old boy was foxy. Somehow he always knew when he was being followed, and he'd lead the boys a wild goose chase. Then they tried to get Homer drunk but it didn't work. He wouldn't take anything stronger than beer, and even a dozen bottles didn't loosen his tongue. I followed the old fellow once—I admit it—but all the good it did was to give me some exercise I didn't want or need.

"One thing was sure. Old Homer had found a cache of money taken from some old shipwreck. I read one time about five Spanish galleons that were wrecked on the reef of Key Largo back in 1767 during a storm. The story said that more than a million in gold and silver was lost. If you're asking me I'd say that old Homer Ludwig found a part of it, at least.

"One day I stopped by Homer's shack and made a proposition. I told him I'd help him dig up all the treasure on shares, and see that he got a decent house to live in and a new boat, but he wasn't interested. He said he was doing all right the way things were. I gathered that his idea of living high on the hog was to have plenty of sardines on hand, and to be left alone. Some of the people on Largo thought the old boy was crazy, and maybe he was a bit touched, but he was harmless. Me? I just figured he was getting childish.

"One day in September of 1909 old Homer got in his boat and started hoisting the sail. A couple of fishermen told him he'd better stay ashore because a bad storm was building up. But the old fellow wouldn't listen. He shoved off and headed north—I guess he was making another trip to Miami, but he never got there. That night the storm came howling up the keys, and Homer was never heard of again. The secret of where the treasure was hidden went with him. Somewhere on Key Largo the rest of that old Spanish treasure is waiting for a second finder. If I had any idea of about where it might be I'd go back there and do a little digging myself."

And so ended the story of Homer Ludwig, a man of simple habits and simple wants. He had no desire to be rich, no desire for the finer things of life. All he wanted was peace and quiet—and a constant supply of sardines in olive oil.

On the Trail of Pirate Treasure

Time 1920-1940   *Place: Tampa Bay to Key West*

HERE WAS A TIME when it didn't take much more than a mild rumor, or an old fashioned hunch, to get me started off on a treasure hunt. I was a young fellow back in those days, and I had all the optimism that goes with youth. Why work all your life to save up a little stake for old age, when by a digging—in the right place— you might unearth enough pirate treasure to take care of everything to the end of your days.

There were quite a few times when I let my regular work go, and piled shovel, water jug and a sandwich or two, into my car or boat, and sallied forth a treasure hunting. My wife took a decidedly dim view of the whole thing. She didn't want the sun and sweat and insects that go with exploring in the bays and coves, and she didn't want to stay home alone, either. Being a very practical person, the good wife always insisted that there was no substitute for a steady job for the person who wanted to get ahead in this world. Perhaps she was right, but at the same time it just goes to show that she didn't understand what goes on inside a fellow when he's been bitten by the treasure bug.

I was almost forty before I finally gave up my treasure hunting sorties, and settled down to write about pirates, the sea, animals, and tales of the early Florida settlers. I decided—with some nagging help from my wife—that I was getting too far along in life to go around digging holes in the wrong places, and let my typewriter gather dust. Besides, and this is true, I have found that on the average you can make more out of pirate treasure by writing about it, than you can by digging.

Still, I wouldn't want to discourage any young man—or woman—from going treasure hunting. If it's in your blood you will do well to play along until you work it out of your system. You'll be happier that way, and who knows? You might find something. Others have. In my humble opinion there's a lot more treasure still buried in the ground than has ever been found. For every large cache there are probably a half dozen small ones, and even a small find might be worth a few thousand dollars on today's market.

When it comes to finding treasure there's no substitute for being the first on the scene with a shovel. Several times I arrived where I'm sure treasure must have been, but got there just a bit too late. In short, I was the late bird who missed the early worm.

Back in 1936 a family moved into the house next door, and one evening the lady, who had recently taught in the one room school at the little fishing village of St. James at the south end of Big Pine Island, happened to mention that one of her pupils had discovered a rock with the carving of a pirate ship on it. She hadn't seen the rock, but the children said there were some letters carved into the stone, and an arrow pointing to the east.

The next morning saw me rattling along the dusty shelled road down the length of Pine Island, to interview the brother and sister the teacher had mentioned. In response to my eager question the boy and girl, who were about 12 and 14, said the "picture rock", as they called it, was about a mile or so up the beach, then another mile or so up a long slough towards the center of the island. Both readily agreed to be my guide, and on the hottest part of a July afternoon we set out without thinking of taking any drinking water.

The children turned out to be very poor estimators of distance. We tramped at least two miles along the beach under a cloudless sky, then went at least three miles up the soggy bed of the tidal slough. I was soon in far worse shape than the girl or boy. My tongue was like a wad of cotton, but the treasure hunting fever was still strong, and I forced myself to keep going.

In time—it seemed an age to me—we arrived at a field of huge rocks cropping above the mud of the slough. Some were all of 10 or 12 feet in diameter and flat on top. After a brief search the girl found the "picture rock" and gave a yell. I got up from the rock I'd been resting on, and went to look. To say that I was disappointed is to state it very mildly. The carving of the two-masted ship was far smaller than I had expected; hardly larger than my hand. There were a few letters indented in the rock, and a fair sized arrow pointed to where the trunk of a long dead pine tree stood on the high ground in the medium distance.

I was so miserable from thirst, and so let down by the smallness of the picture on the rock, that all I could think of was to make it back to the nearest house and drink their rain water tank dry. Any more exploring would have to wait for another day.

I let two months go by before I returned to St. James City. On the first cool day of September I put my treasure hunting gear in the back of my car—with a gallon jug of ice water—and made my way back to the "picture rock" without any trouble. As I slogged up the tidal slough I became slowly aware that someone had been that way not long before. There were the outlines of several pair of footprints in the oozy mud, and parallel marks, or lines, along the bed of the tidal wash. It looked like someone had dragged sticks along the slough. I wondered about it, but my suspicions were not aroused until I reached the "picture rock."

On arriving there I saw a stake driven into the sand beside the rock, and from it a long length of carpenter's line sagged off toward the east and the nearby woods. Leaving my jug and gear behind, I set off to follow the chalk line in the direction of the dead pine tree. The line went over a large clump of palmetto and brush, and about half way between the "picture rock" and the dead pine, I came to a large hole dug under some hefty palmetto roots.

I stood there and looked around in surprise. Close by I saw the fresh cut stumps of two 4-inch pines, with the bright chips and the green branches spread about. What had happened seemed plain enough. A couple of men had dug up something heavy—too heavy to carry—and had cut the pine poles to form a drag. The "find" had been lashed to the poles and dragged along the slough to a waiting boat where the slough emptied into Pine Island Sound. Who were the lucky men? I made inquiry among the fishermen and residents of St. James. No one remembered of having seen strangers, or a strange boat off the mouth of the slough. What had been taken, and who took it, is a mystery to this day. I have always blamed myself for not going back sooner, in spite of the hot August days, and making an all out search for the treasure which must have been there. All I would have had to do would have been to follow the arrow carved in the rock, and to have taken soundings along a straight line between the "picture rock" and the big dead tree.

A popular figure around Fort Myers for about 35 years was a man named Thomas H. Phillips. He was born in Pocomoke City, Maryland, sold some of his patents to the General Electric Co., was associated for a time with the Sperry Gyroscope Co., and came to Fort Myers in 1918. I knew him, and was his friend from 1920 until his death just a short time ago. I knew Tom when he was "in the

Greek Sponge Diver recovering a chest from an old wreck off
Boca Grande Pass

chips" as he used to say, and I knew him when he was
about as "flat" as the under side of a flounder. I never
knew a man who had as many ups and downs as good old
Tom, but he came out on top in the end.

Tom was an inventor at heart, and was always working
on some scheme to do something useful, and do it better.
From time to time he got me to help him with some of his
ideas, and he had some good ones. That he made more out
of his real estate operations than he did from patents, was
due partly to the times, and partly to his ability to see into
the future. Tom had a ready smile, and he always had
something to cause a laugh. It was either the very latest

joke, or a trick gadget to catch the unwary. Everybody liked Tom.

Back in the 1930s Tom Phillips was bitten by the treasure bug, and he invented an electronic treasure finder. I helped him wind some of the delicate coils for his first models. In time one of the popular science magazines published an article on Tom's treasure finder, and he was soon swamped with inquiries from all over the world. Seeing the profit possibilities, Tom prepared blueprints showing "how to make your own", and he sold the diagrams and instructions for something like $2 each. Small ads in a few magazines brought in orders for a long period, and Tom was kept busy mailing out the instruction kits.

One day shortly after Tom had completed a new working model of his treasure finder, he came to me with a proposition. Back about 1900 there had lived an old cattleman, a recluse, in a log cabin on the edge of a cypress stand about five miles from town. The old cattleman, Matt McKay, was known to have sold many a head of his cattle to the Spanish Government in the days before the Spanish-American War, and to have received his pay in gold at the pens at Punta Rassa. What old Matt did with his gold was never known, save that he didn't trust banks and would have nothing to do with them.

"It used to be rumored that old Matt McKay buried his gold under his cabin," Tom told me on this particular day, "so I went to where his cabin used to be, and put my new finder to work. Guess what! There's an indication of metal in a big circle. Help me to dig this afternoon and I'll cut you in for a share of all we find."

I was not only willing, but eager to get in on the deal. That same afternoon we followed a sand trail through the flat woods to where Matt's cabin had been. The logs had burned up in a grass fire years before, but there was still a rough outline of where the old batchelor had spent his last years. Tom unlimbered his treasure finder, moved over to where you could see a slight depression in the ground, and let me listen to the earphones. I could hear the noise level rise and fall as the finder passed around the edges of the depression. There was no indication of metal when the finder moved to the middle of the low place.

"There's something funny going on," said Tom. "Whoever heard of treasure being buried in a circle? Well, here we are—let's start digging."

I took first turn with the shovel, and before I'd gone very deep I scraped against a cypress plank. "Hot dog!" I thought, "Maybe this is a part of a chest." I went a little deeper and the shovel hit metal. I was sure we had something. I dug a little more and found I had hit iron—a rusty band it looked like. I thought it might be an iron bound wooden chest at first, but it wasn't.

After a little more digging around on the other side of the low place, we slowly came to realize what we had found. It seemed that old Matt got his water from a dug well, but to keep the well from caving in and filling up he had put down a cypress water tank, with the iron hoops on the inside instead of the outside. So that's all we had for our trouble; the knowledge that the place contained some slowly rotting cypress staves and three or four rusting iron hoops. We went back to town and called it a day. I'd had my high hopes dashed many a time before, so I didn't take it too hard. I always figured that the very next time might be my lucky day.

There came a time—some twenty-five years later—when for a short period I experienced the same type of thrill that I imagine must be felt by all successful treasure seekers. My hopes were soon dashed, as it turned out, but for a few minutes I was certain that I had come across a treasure trove left by Gasparilla, Caesar le Grande or one of the other buccaneers of the seventeen or eighteen hun-

The day in question started like many other days, for I was getting some exercise by working on my grounds, which once were a part of Thomas Edison's Florida estate. A cold spell had killed one of my giant coconut palms, and I took it upon myself to dig up the roots and bole, and fill in the resulting hole. This was no mean job for a large, mature coconut palm can have as many as 5,000 slender but fibrous roots, and the base of the trunk was almost three feet across. I dug a trench around the dead palm, and then went to work with an axe to chop the tough roots.

Without any warning I felt the axe strike something more solid than roots and dirt, and when I paused to look down into the deepening trench I saw bright metal. I fell to my knees to get a better look, and I could hardly breathe for the lump in my throat. SILVER! ! ! My sharp blade had sliced into a large chunk of metal, and from the cut bright metal gleamed up at me. The silver, or whatever it was, proved to be surrounded with palm roots, and only after some frantic effort with shovel and pinch bar was I able to remove the slab from the hole, The metal—twelve by eighteen inches in size, and quite thick, had obviously been buried in the ground for many a year, for the 60 foot palm had grown on top of it.

Well, my heavy chunk of metal turned out to be pure lead instead of silver, and brought a day's wages when sold to a junk dealer. Both the lead and the coconut palm had been planted there during the years Thomas Edison had owned the property, but why I do not know. It is a mystery that may never be solved.

Treasure — Thirty Fathoms Deep

Time: 1938   *Place*: *Tarpon Springs*

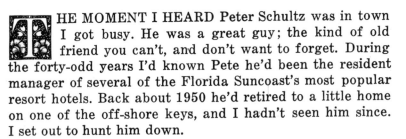

HE MOMENT I HEARD Peter Schultz was in town I got busy. He was a great guy; the kind of old friend you can't, and don't want to forget. During the forty-odd years I'd known Pete he'd been the resident manager of several of the Florida Suncoast's most popular resort hotels. Back about 1950 he'd retired to a little home on one of the off-shore keys, and I hadn't seen him since. I set out to hunt him down.

When I finally caught up with Pete he was sitting in the lobby of the Bradford Hotel, and idly watching the hectic flow of US 41 traffic up and down First Street in Fort Myers. I slumped into a leather chair beside Pete, and for the next hour we relived the old days and spoke of future plans. In time he mentioned my latest paperback novel; a tale of pirates and buried treasure in the days when Florida still belonged to Spain.

"I read it," Pete informed me protestingly, "and it kept me up all night—I couldn't put it down!" He took time to fire up another cigarette, then rested a hand on my sleeve. "Did I ever get to tell you about the Greek diver who found a fortune on the bottom of the Gulf near Boca Grande?"

"N-o—," I said, thinking back, "but it sounds interesting. Go ahead—spill it."

"Well," Pete began, "I know this sounds like another of those cockeyed yarns, but it's the truth, so help me! The first half comes from my personal knowledge, and my son Jim—you remember him—will swear to the other half. I'll give you the facts—the way it actually happened—then maybe you can use it in one of those books you write."

I took a moment to open the pocket notebook I always carry, and unlimbered my ball point pen. With me note taking is a habit.

"This happened about twenty years ago, while I was managing the Mallorca Island Inn up the coast, north of St. Petersburg," Pete began. "Every now and then I'd have a guest or two—the adventurous kind—who'd get me to arrange a diving trip on one of the Greek sponge boats at Tarpon Springs. What they wanted was to see what the bottom of the Gulf of Mexico looked like, and they'd come back with some big hunks of fan coral, a few strange shells, and some live sponges that smelled to high heaven inside a day or two.

"The diver I usually hired to take charge of these dudes was a young Greek named Alexander Pappadakus. He was Number 1 diver on the sponge boat, *STAVROS III*, owned by Captain Carrapellous, a crusty old fellow who'd been in the States for thirty years and still couldn't speak English.

"The way I met this Alex was through my son. The boys were about the same age, and my son Jim had hired the Greek to give him some diving lessons. You couldn't help liking the tall, good looking Greek. He had the build of an Apollo, and the only blemishes on his entire body were a tattoo on the back of his right hand, and V-shaped scar

Pirates unearthing treasure on a Florida key

on his right cheek. Like so many of the Greeks born in the Old Country, he spoke English with a broad accent.

"I'd been doing business with Alex for some five or six years," Pete rambled on, "when he came into my office late one night. I could tell that he was excited about something, and he came right to the point.

" 'Meester Pete,' he began in his Greek way, 'you good friend! You do me beeg favor, no?' Before I had time to speak he started to talk fast. 'You loan me five thousand dollar, Meester Pete! Is important, you bet! Then I buy good sponge boat, the *Athena X*! Is good reasons why I need boat, Meester Pete. I tell you, but you no tell—I find monies—plenty monies, old monies. Is secret, you bet! You loan me monies, Meester Pete, an' I pay back fast. With big interest monies, too, you bet!'

" ' Now wait!' I said to Alex. 'Let's get this straight. You want to borrow money to get a boat of your own— but why?'

" 'I telling you, Meester Pete—when dive for sponges I find old wreck—thirty fathoms deep. Inside is old monies —much monies—gold, silver monies, you bet! Is secret— I no telling anybody where is. Is secret, you an me, Meester Pete. You loan me monies—I buy boat. With boat I get beeg monies. Then I pay back with interest. You name and I pay! You will do, Meester Pete?' "

"And you did," I broke in on Peter. He smiled at the memory.

"I did" he said. "It looked foolish on the face of it, but Alex had a way with him. I wrote out a check but didn't let the wife know. I didn't even make Alex sign a note. Somehow I just seemed to know I could trust him. Inside a week I heard that Alex was the new skipper of the *Athena X*, and had sailed out into the Gulf with a green crew he'd picked up in Tampa.

"During the next month the *Athena X* was back in port several times, but the string of sponges dangling from her mast was pitifully small. The dock loafers were betting that Alex would go broke in a jiffy. It served him right, they said, for signing on a crew of landlubbers.

"Six weeks after he'd made the down payment on the boat Alex was back in my office again. There was a desperate gleam in his eyes, and he couldn't keep hands or feet still.

" 'Meester Pete,' he began as soon as we were alone, 'you loan me thousand dollar more, please! Need bad, you bet! Beeg thing is happen soon. You loan me the monies and everything be hokay, you bet!' "

"And you did," I interrupted. Pete took time to fish out another cigarette and light up.

"Yes, but not before I made him answer some questions," Pete replied. "He told me he had to have a power winch for some heavy lifting—said he could get a second-hand one at Key West for five hundred. The rest of the thousand he needed to pay his crew. That was all I could get out of him except the assurance that he'd pay me back with 'beeg interest monies, you bet!' The only thing I could do was to write Alex another check.

"That was the next to the last time I ever saw Alexander Pappadakus," said Peter. "The last time was some two months later, but in the meantime I heard plenty of rumors. Some said Alex was running dope, and others that he was smuggling aliens in from Cuba. I didn't take any stock in either. I didn't figure him for that kind of a chap. Then a guide boat captain told me he'd seen the *Athena X* anchored in deep water a few miles off Gasparilla Island out in the Gulf. He said he saw a boom over the side with heavy cables reaching down into the water, and there was a diver working below. He went close enough to see the air hose and safety line, and the air bubles were breaking the surface."

"So this Greek was working over some old wreck," I broke in. "Do you suppose it could have been the wreck of Gasparilla's pirate ship? The one sank by the *USS Enterprise* in 1821?"

"Could have been," Pete observed. "All I know is that Alex had plenty of cash the last time I saw him. I hardly knew him—the way he was dressed. Instead of the patched dungarees he'd always worn, he was in white flannels, with new two-toned shoes and an expensive sport coat. Yes, and he'd had a haircut. When he walked into my office I thought he was one of the hotel guests—until I took a second look. The next thing I knew he'd tossed some paper money on my desk.

" 'Is what I owe you, Meester Pete,' he grinned. 'I sell boat an' go back to Old Country to see my peeples. Everything is hokay. I say "Goodbye" now.'

"He held out his hand, but instead of taking it I reached and counted the money. There were ten one thousand dollar bills!

" 'Look here!' I said, 'You don't owe me this much. At six percent for about four months you only owe me about $120 in interest, not $4,000.'

" ' I know,' Alex came back, 'but you keep the monies, Meester Pete! Is hokay with me. You good friend an' I no take back. I got plenty monies left, you bet!' With that he almost ran from the hotel, and left the money on my desk.

"That was the last I ever saw of Alexander Pappadakus," said Pete, "and the rest of the story happened to my son, Jim. He joined the Air Force back in 1943, and decided to stay on when the war was over. In 1950 he was spending a thirty-day leave in L. A. and one day he happened to pull up at a red light alongside a foreign sport car. It wasn't one of those pesky, insignificant puddle-jumpers, but a real job about the size of a Cadillac—and expensive. Who sits at the wheel of the flashy car but Alex Pappadakus. At least it was a dead ringer for Alex. Jim looked for the V-shaped scar—and there it was!

" 'Hi, there, Alex!' Jim yelled out loud. He saw the driver of the foreign car give a start. Just then the light turned green, and the guy who looked like Alex put a heavy foot on the gas and shot away.

"About a week later Jim spotted the same big, red sport car parked at a Drive-In out on the Strip, and he walked over. The fellow who looked like Alex had two girls with him—big busty blondes who looked like movie starlets.

" 'Hello, Alex!' Jim said. 'You remember me —? Jim Schultz—from Tarpon Springs?'

" 'Is a mistake,' said the Greek. 'Name is no Alex—name is Fredie—Fredie Pappas. Is not right, girls?' "

" 'You're mistaken, mister,' said one of the blondes, giving Jim the eye at the same time. 'He's Fredie, all right.' The other girl nodded agreement.

The Greek's arm was draped along the back of the seat, and Jim spotted the tattoo mark on the back of the right hand. Then he gave a close look at the man's face. The scar was just as he remembered it. There was practically no chance for a mistake.

" 'Well,' said Jim at last, 'you're a dead ringer for a sponge diver I used to know in Florida—even to the tattoo and scar on your cheek.'

" 'Don't know any fellow is name Pappadakus,' the Greek almost shouted. 'Be good sport, meester—no make trouble for me! Is hokay?' Just then the curb hop removed the tray from the car door, and the Greek stepped on the starter. As the car rolled away the man who looked like Alex gave Jim a broad wink, and the flossie who'd been giving Jim the eye waved behind the Greek's back.

"That's about all I know," said Pete, "except that Jim tried to do a little investigating. All he could find out before his leave was up was that the fellow who called himself Fredie Pappas was well heeled, and had quite a reputation for being a playboy. No one seemed to know his background. He'd arrived in L. A. some dozen years before, and started throwing money around. He played the races a lot, but wasn't mixed up in any of the rackets. The police didn't have a thing on him."

Pete fell silent and I thought it over for a moment. "So you think this Greek fellow, Alex, really found a fortune in the Gulf," I said at last.

"There's no doubt in my mind," Pete said. "Everything ties in—he'd probably run across the sunken wreck while diving for sponges, kept it a secret, bought his own boat— with the money I loaned him—and brought up the treasure. It was probably Spanish gold and silver. After that he just cashed in and skipped out."

"How much do you suppose he got?" I asked.

"I wouldn't know," said Pete. "A hundred thousand? A million, five million—maybe ten million? Your guess is as good as mine?"

"What bothers me," I said, "is why he went to California, changed his name, and refused to acknowledge old friends. You'd think he was afraid of something."

"Sure he was afraid!" Pete answered. "Florida has a treasure trove law—a share of all you find goes to the State. Then there's the Internal Revenue Department— they want a deep cut of anything you find. Add the two together and you might not have much left. Oh, Alex was a smart young Greek the way I have it figured." Pete sighed and hunted for another cigarette. "Under the same circumstances," he said between puffs, "I'd have been tempted to do just what Alex did. How about you?"

The Missing Gold of Useppa Island

Time: 1895   *Place*: *Useppa Island*

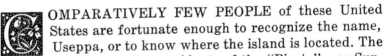OMPARATIVELY FEW PEOPLE of these United States are fortunate enough to recognize the name, Useppa, or to know where the island is located. The fortunate few are either residents of the "Pirate"—or Suncoast—islands off Florida's southwest coast, or else devotees of the art of angling for that greatest of salt water fish, the Silver King Tarpon. For many a year Useppa, located as it is near the deep waters of Boca Grande Pass, has been inhabited in season by wealthy sportsmen and women, but this was not always true.

There was a time—some one hundred and fifty years ago—when pirates roamed over the little isle, and once made it a prison for a dainty sixteen year old Spanish girl of noble blood. Her name was Josefa Inez de Mayorga; she was the youngest daughter of a former Viceroy of Mexico, and she was brutally murdered by the great Gasparilla when she spurned his attempts at love making. On this picturesque isle, too, the aging Gasparilla is supposed to have hidden one of his copper lined treasure casks.

Useppa is but one of many islands reaching from Charlotte Harbor to San Carlos Bay—and beyond—where pir-

ates of the early 1800s established fact or legend, but so
far as this writer knows Useppa is one of the few places
where pirate treasure in any vast amount has been discovered. Even in this case the names of the finders are unknown, as is the actual value of the treasure. Here is the
full story as it came to me.

Back in the gay nineties, a Mr. John M. Roach of Chicago, began spending a part of each winter at the town
of Fort Myers in South Florida. In those days the means of
travel was by rail to the village of Punta Gorda on the
Peace River, then by paddle wheel steamer down Charlotte
Harbor, through the length of Pine Island Sound—passing
close to Useppa Island—and up the Caloosahatchee to Fort
Myers.

Each time he passed Useppa Mr. Roach became more
entranced by the elevation and natural beauty of the verdant isle, and at last bought the entire island for a winter
home for his family. He built a small cottage the first year,
and established a younger brother there to supervise and
carry on the development work.

One evening just before sunset the young Mr. Roach
was sitting alone, admiring the glowing colors the dipping
sun was painting on clouds and bay alike, when he spied
a small schooner coming in from the Gulf. At dusk the
strange craft anchored off the island, and two roughly
dressed, short spoken men came ashore in a small boat.
They asked nothing more than permission refill their water
casks from a small spring near the middle of the island.
This spring, the only one in the area, had been a stopping
place for passing boats for many, many a year, and the
request aroused no suspicion in young Roach's mind. Since
it was almost dark, the men stated that they would wait
until morning to take the water aboard, and returned to
the schooner.

Young Roach was awakened several times during the
night by strange sounds—like the clink of metal against
metal—but each time went back to sleep without investi-

"Pirates burying a treasure chest on a Florida key."

gating. He awoke early in the morning, and was surprised to see that the visiting schooner was already gone. When he carried his water bucket to the spring he had an even greater surprise. He was amazed to see a large hole dug into the bank, with fresh piled sand all around. In the very bottom of the hole he saw the oblong imprint of a box with metal bindings. The dimensions of the imprint were about those of a large seaman's chest. Judging by the depths of the surrounding footprints in the loose sand, the box or chest must have been of considerable weight.

Convinced from his rapid examination that a treasure of great value had been removed during the night, young Roach ran to the house for his rifle, and took off in his fast sailing sharpie. He decided the schooner had probably gone on down the Sound, and he spent the rest of the day searching as far south as San Carlos Bay without sighting a trace of the missing schooner. That ended the affair as far as the Roaches were concerned.

Years later the island was bought by the late Barron Collier, New York advertising millionaire, and he built a large inn and group of cottages for the tarpon fraternity. In 1916, while a new golf course was being established on Useppa, the treasure hole near the spring was rediscovered. It had never been refilled, and since it was slightly to the left of the No. 2 fairway, it was decided to leave it there as a sand trap. When the greens-keeper was raking the accumulated leaves and trash from the old treasure hole he saw several bright spots among the debris. On examination they proved to be gold coins, octagonal in shape, and about the size of a dime. The design was said to have been of a two-headed eagle, with crown and spears, and bearing the date of 1761. This small find seems to have verified young Roach's story—if verification was ever needed.

According to the very earliest settlers, and to government maps made before 1850, the name of this island was given as Josefa's Island, in memory no doubt, of the little Spanish girl who was murdered there. Since about 1850 the island has been called Useppa, but no matter it's name, it is a bit of land steeped in history, and well worth your visit.

Treasure's Where You Find It

Time: Then and Now .. Place: Charlotte Harbor Region

OULD YOU LIKE TO BE a treasure hunter? Well, good! The desire to unearth Gasparilla's golden loot, or to bring up a heap of pieces-of-eight from the coral encrusted hulk of an old Spanish galleon is the basic equipment you need—that, and a pick and shovel, and a dependable skin diving outfit. There's millions of acres of land and water bottoms here in Florida, where you can dig, sink a shaft, operate a dredge, or do a bit of diving. No one is going to stop you unless you get on private property. If you work, sweat and have the needed equipment; if you use good judgment in selecting your location; if you have proper financing, and if you have the luck of the Irish—then, my dear fellow, you're rich.

It should go without saying that an accurate, dependable, authentic and bona-fide treasure map — with "X" marks-the-spot — is a big help to a treasure hunter. Personally, I've never had intimate contact with such a map, but I know several men who claim to have them. Maybe they do, but there is one thing bothering me. What I can't figure out is this; if they have this authentic treasure information, why is it that they aren't living any higher on the hog than I am? If I had an honest-to-gosh, sure-fire treasure map I'd be rich before you could say "Scat".

Treasure hunters have been active along the Florida coast these many years, and I doubt not but what some of the claims of treasure finds I've heard about are true. In fact I'm sure they are. I have good reason to think that some legitimate "finds" have never appeared in the public press. Why? Because some treasure finders are naturally shy about their personal affairs; some fear the rightful property owner—or the State—may try to collect a share in the loot, and then there is that monster known as the Internal Revenue Service. After they take their cut out of any sizable treasure trove the finder would probably end up with the short end of the stick.

During my many years along the Suncoast I've heard of many a person, or persons, setting out on treasure hunts, especially on the keys, and they weren't all harebrained expeditions, either. Back in September of 1940 the Fort Myers News-Press ran a front page story headlined, "GAS-PARILLA'S PIRATE GOLD SOUGHT NEAR BOCA GRANDE — Treasure Hunt Opens With Draglines And Big Motor Pumps." The names of the partners mentioned in this enterprise included that of a well known lawyer, the president of a bank, a Chicago millionaire, and a wealthy New York City sewer contractor.

Another treasure hunter told me that he had seen the huge holes dug by the power equipment in the vicinity of Charlotte Harbor, but what they found—if anything—was never reported in the papers. Not long ago I asked the treasure hunting lawyer's law partner what had been found, but he claimed not to know. All the members of the syndicate have since died, so the answer may never be known.

Another treasure hunter who claims to have a real treasure map and electronic finder, told me that he had prospected the area around Cape Haze and some of the inner islands. At one place he found some old graves surrounded by brass rails removed from some ship. The graves gave an indication of buried metal, and after some digging

A prisoner fights for his life after uncovering an old treasure chest
at Marco Island

some silver jewelry of Mexican design was found among the bones. The bracelets and rings were so badly oxidized that they crumbled at the touch, and were of little value.

When the bones were examined by a competent authority it was established that they were those of young women, and several of the skulls showed bullet holes. It was considered likely that the women had been murdered by Gasparilla, or some of his men, about the time the pirates were preparing to leave Florida for good.

I recently interviewed an elderly man at Punta Gorda who sailed the waters of Charlotte Harbor for fifty years. He claimed that he knew where Gasparilla had hidden some of his loot, and he told me about once finding the graves of perhaps a dozen people on the island of Cara Pelau. He said the graves had been marked when he first discovered them, but as years passed someone had taken the brass stobs away.

"Gasparilla didn't hide all his gold in the ground," the old gentleman told me in all seriousness. "Some of it is under water," he continued, "and I know just about where. Say, you don't know where I can borrow a diving suit, do you?"

For some years it has been claimed that one of the Boca Grande Harbor Pilots knows the location of Gasparilla's sunken vessel. According to various news reports there have been efforts to salvage the contents of this ship, but each time the changing tide has shifted the sands, and defeated all efforts to uncover the hull.

As recently as 1956 a story with a St. Petersburg dateline stated that: "TREASURE HUNTER HEADS FOR ISLANDS NEAR FORT MYERS." This party, whom I later interviewed while they were restocking their larder at Fort Myers Beach, were fitted out with a shallow draft houseboat, diving equipment and electronic gear. When I last heard of the expedition they were at work at Mound Key and what luck they had I do not know.

Another treasure map owner, and a darn nice fellow

to know and talk with, is Captain Ernie Hall, the writer of the "Along The Waterfront" column in the *Fort Myers News-Press*. He is a veritable storehouse of pirate, treasure and sailing lore, some of which is all true, some perhaps just half true, and the rest is on the downright humorous side. Talk to Captain Hall for a minute or less and you'll see what I mean. The following is one of Captain Ernie's serious offerings:—

"For many a year," he told me, "there lived in a cabin on Shell Creek, an old Spaniard named Juan Gonzalez— (not to be confused with Juan Gomez)—who claimed he had pirated with Jose' Gaspar up to the time the racket was broken up by Captain Kearney and the *USS Enterprise*. He escaped to the mainland, settled on Shell Creek near Lettuce Lake, and from then on always seemed to have a few gold coins in his ragged pockets. He wasn't rich, mind you, but always had enough, year after year, to supply his simple needs. They say he claimed, the few times he was in a talking mood, to know where Gasparilla had stashed away a copper cask, worth up to several millions, at a place near the shore of Lettuce Lake.

"I don't know the exact year," Captain Ernie admits, "but it must have been soon after the Civil War when old Gonzalez made a deal with a couple of cattlemen up Punta Gorda way. He was to take these men to Lettuce Lake and show them exactly where to dig. The money was to be put in a safe place to the old pirate's credit for as long as he lived, and at his death all that remained was to go to the two cattlemen. Well, according to a letter left by one of these men, a time was set to meet at the old pirate's shack, but when they arrived with a skiff on an oxcart as per agreement, it was no go. The aging Spaniard was ill with one of his frequent 'spells', and he told the men to come back in a couple of days when he would be in better shape. Yes, you've guessed it. When the cattlemen went back a few days later the old pirate was dead on the heap of rags he called a bed.

"As soon as the men had old Gonzalez permanently planted—toes up in a Christian manner—they tore his shack apart to see what they could find. All told it didn't amount to much — a jar a third full of old coins — some silver, some gold—worth about three or four hundred dollars, and a couple of charts, crudely etched or engraved on copper plates. They were supposed to show the location of the buried treasure.

"Far as I know," Captain Ernie continued, "this treasure has never been found. I've seen exact copies of both charts—photostats—and the story seems to be authentic. If you want to go looking for it I'll give you all the help I can. Of course I can't pinpoint it for you, but I can tell you something about the equipment you should take along on your treasure safari. Besides a shovel and electronic gear, you'll need a fifth of rye—for snake bites,what else? —and a hammock for afternoon naps—so's you can 'dream' up ways to spend the loot. Then, too, you'll need a good stout gunny sack—one with no holes in the corners. You'd look mighty foolish hiking back from your treasure find, and dribbling doubloons, escudos, sovereigns or pieces-of-eight along the path behind you.

'There's just one more thing I ought to tell you," said the Captain with a twinkle showing, "and that's to dig, dig, and keep on digging until . . . What's that? You want to know where to start digging . . . ?" The good Captain scratched his head and thought for a moment. "Oh, you might as well dig anyplace," he said. "After all's said and done, it isn't where you dig that's so all fired important. It's finding the good old yellow stuff that really counts."

The Curse of Cara Pelau

Time: Then and Now   *Place: Charlotte Harbor*

 HE ISLAND OF CARA PELAU, or Cayo Pelau as it is named on some Government maps, is an isle with a history, and steeped in mystery. The odd shaped island lies some three miles inside Charlotte Harbor from the city of Boca Grande on Gasparilla Island, but few are the people who have visited it in recent years. Those who have beached a boat there, and have wandered over the upland portions of the isle, have returned to recount some strange tales. Of these we shall speak later.

Cayo Pelau, or Cara Pelau as you wish, was not always the deserted place it appears to be today. If we are to believe history as it has been handed down from generation to generation, this island was once the location of "Low Town", where the pirate, Gasparilla, sent his common pirates to do their howling, drinking and wenching between their forays in the Caribbean and along the Spanish Main.

History has it that Don Jose' Gaspar, or Gasparilla, lived like a Spanish gentleman when he was home from the sea. It is said that the Casa Primero in the pirate village of Boca Grande, was done in rare woods and tapestries, all taken from plundered vessels, and that he dressed himself and his ladies of quality in looted satins and silks.

During Gasparilla's periods ashore he spent his time in reading stolen books, for he had a scholarly mind, or in listening to one of his captive ladies play the lute or harpsichord. For these pursuits he needed peace in his house and quiet on the island, so he banished those of his men who delighted in carousing and drunkeness, to the huts and hovels of Low Town on nearby Cara Pelau. Thus the two pirate hangouts were soon known as High Town, where Gasparilla and his top officers lived with their women and servants, and Low Town where the common sailormen pirates gambled, drank, howled and yowled, and played at love making, both by day and by night.

There is good reason to believe that many a small cache of pirate loot was buried in the sands of Cayo Pelau in the years between 1800 and 1821, and much of it may still be there. From time to time the loot, or profits of the enterprise, were divided into shares, and after that it was each man on his own. Since there was so little honor among thieves, each man would hide most of his share in some secret place. If the man was killed in a battle at sea and did not return, then the plunder he buried under some tree or rock is still there today. Some of this treasure has been found by the use of electronic equipment, but it is reasonable to suppose that the great majority of such hidden loot still awaits a finder.

Of late years a number of treasure hunters have visited Cara Pelau, but the ones I have talked with have, strangely enough, all told the same story. They agree that the island is haunted, bewitched, or suffering from some unknown curse. They have reported finding man-made caves on the higher ground, now mostly filled with sand and debris, where people once lived or loot was buried.

The wife of one treasure hunter, while walking on what appeared to be perfectly solid ground, suddenly broke through the coarse sod and fell into a hole up to her armpits. The young woman wrenched her back and had to be carried back to the boat. When the husband returned to the island about a month later, to do some digging where his wife had plunged into the hole, he could not find the spot. He did discover that fresh earth had been turned over in five spots in that vicinity, but which had been the scene of his wife's accident he could not tell.

"There is a curse on Cara Pelau," a well known treasure hunter living in Orlando told me recently. "I drove to the village of Placida three different times," he continued, "and each time I couldn't hire a guide to take me to Cara Pelau. Each time, when they found out where I wanted to go, they made some lame excuse for not being able to make the trip. It wasn't a case of money—they just seemed scared to go to Cara Pelau.

"The fourth time I hauled my own boat and outboard on a trailer, and I got to Cara Pelau without any trouble. The trouble only started after I got there. I had two treasure finders with me, and I'd tested them both thoroughly before starting on the trip. At home I have some old coins and bits of metal buried at various levels under my back yard, and I always make sure the gadgets are working before I start on a field trip.

"Well, to make the story short, neither of those finders would give off a "peep" when I tried to use them on the island. I even threw my jackknife on top of the ground, and the darn thing wouldn't give an indication when held an inch above it. It was the weirdest thing you ever saw. I thought I'd had it about then, but there was more to come.

"When we went back to the boat to get our lunch we found it half full of water, and our lunch basket was afloat. How the water got into the boat I never found out, for after we bailed it out it never leaked any more. You figure that one out. So then we had to go hungry. Who wants to eat sandwiches that have been soaked in spilled gas, oil, the remains of dead shrimp and crab bait from under the floor boards, and a boat half full of salt water?

"We didn't know it then, but the worst was still to happen. We started back towards Placida, but before we'd gone a hundred yards from Cara Pelau the motor froze up —tight. There was plenty of oil mixed with the gas, but the pistons were locked tighter than a loan shark's heart. There was only one thing we could do—spend the rest of the afternoon paddling and poling the boat back across the bay. What made it worse, and a lot more uncomfortable, was that a sudden squall came up when fair weather had been predicted, and we were all about half drowned.

"When I got back to Orlando the first thing I did was to test my finders in my back yard. Both were working perfectly, and haven't given any trouble since. Then when I went to work on my outboard the next day, it wasn't stuck any more. I ran it for an hour in a barrel of water, and it's been behaving ever since. There's a curse on Cara Pelau," he finished, "and neither you, nor anyone else, can tell me any different."

Another indefatigable treasure hunter from the Florida East Coast also ran into difficulties on Cara Pelau. Under the date of May 28th, 1958, he wrote as follows:

" . . . We made a trip two weeks ago to Cayo Pelau, but did not find the four graves—think they were covered up in rank growth of weeds and vines. Found a burial mound a little further on with bones and holes galore, but just as we found it down came a cold front and we had to retreat to our boat where the kicker refused to start. Luckily we had a spare 1½ horse kicker along, and managed to limp back to Placida in a driving rain. Last time we were here the motor threw the propellor, and we had to be towed by a fish boat. Maybe Gasparilla don't want anyone messing around where one of his wives is buried.

Pirates burying a Treasure Chest at Mound Key

"I do know for a fact that my "bobber" was working strongly before going to the island, even on "map dowsing" when I was in one room and my partner was in another room and moved a ruler over the chart, but when we got to Cayo Pelau it never budged. In fact it went practically dead for two weeks and fouled up a Texas treasure trip for me. Now it has regained most of its power, but only about three-fourths as good as originally. There's something wrong at Cayo Pelau, and as the Frenchman says, 'It makes one furiously to think'. If the truth is known I guess I'm about half afraid to go back there. Can't tell what might happen next."

The Yellow Gold of Black Island

Time: 1920   *Place*: *Estero Bay*

APTAIN MADDOX, back in the years when I knew him well, was the skipper of the *Caloosa Belle*, a dirty and malodorous inter-island freight boat. "Mad Maddox", the islanders from Port Tampa to Key West used to call him, and with some reason. They figured he was a mite crazy on the subjects of pirates and buried gold. Given a listener or two, the old man would spin yarn upon yarn, about Gasparilla, Black Augustus, Captain Baker who sailed under Gasparilla, and other bloody pirates who used the Gulf Coast islands as hideouts in the days when the Floridas belonged to Spain.

If the old captain wasn't telling of some pirate's black deeds, then he was sure to be spilling tales of treasure chests weighted down with jewels, doubloons, escudos, or Mexican minted pieces-of-eight. Either that, or he was telling of wrecked galleons—the plate ships of old Spain.

The *Caloosa Belle* and old Captain Maddox were never far apart, and strange to say, they both ended their long careers the same day, and almost to the very hour. While the remains of the old fellow were being planted—as I recall it was in June of 1924—the *Caloosa Belle* was burning to the waterline near the pass at the south end of Casey Key up in Sarasota County.

My first meeting with the leathery-faced skipper of the *Caloosa Belle* was in the early spring of 1920. I was a youngster then, just out of the army, with vinegar in my blood and a lust for adventure in my mind. A fruit company's ad in a Pittsburgh newspaper offered jobs picking and packing oranges in Florida, and the next day I shipped out for the village of Estero on the fringe of the Everglades. The railroad ended at Fort Myers in those days, and the last lap of my journey was aboard the *Caloosa Belle.*

We left Fort Myers with a deck load of crate material and sacked fertilizer, and by late afternoon the engines were laboring against the tide in the swash channel crossing Estero Bay. I had never seen a more tropical setting. A hundred-odd mangrove covered islands dotted the blue-green waters of this vast inlet, with fringes of coconut palms here and there. A few pelicans dived straight necked, into the limpid depths in search of young and unwary mullet.

I remember spending that day squatting on the narrow deck in the shade of the pilot house, listening to Captain Maddox telling lurid tales of pirates and outlaws in times past. He spoke of Panther Key John, a former pirate who died by drowning in 1900 at the ripe age of 122, and of Black Angustus, a bloody butcher who had been one of Gasparilla's top gunners. He told of others, too, but it was not until near dusk that he mentioned a subject that brought me to quick attention.

"See that island with the hump on it's back?" he asked suddenly, pointing his pipe stem towards the center of the bay. "That's Mound Key, son," he explained. "The hog's back is an old Indian burial mound—full of bones, arrowheads and other Indian junk. When the pirates took over these parts they used to hide their plunder in some of these mounds—where it was easy to find it again. I know that's true," Captain Maddox added as an afterthought, "cause I found some myself—right in that mound!"

"Sure enough?" I remember exclaiming. I got to my feet for a better view. The mound looked grim, almost sinister, in the gathering dusk. Still, I was interested. "What did you find?" I asked in a single breath, "was it pirate gold?"

Captain Maddox nodded. "Back 'bout 1880 it was— when I was little more'n a boy. I was living on Estero Island then, and I rowed over there one Sunday to see what I could find. I dug me four good sized holes, and in the last one I found a fancy silver box—like a jewel case. Inside was a man's gold ring, two crosses—one silver and one gold, a handful of hand hammered gold beads, and a lump of rough melted gold. This last was 'bout the size of my thumb, and a jewelry store fellow down at Key West gave me six hundred dollars for the lot."

"Do you think there's more treasure buried there?" I asked with sudden interest.

"Most likely," said the skipper. "What I found was probably some common pirate's share of the loot. When the loot was divided among the men—share and share alike —each man had to hide his plunder to keep some other pirate from stealing it, and if the fellow was killed or captured—why then the loot he buried is still there where he left it. For every big cache of pirate plunder among these islands, there's probably a hundred little individual caches stashed away, and waiting to be found."

For the next month the thought of possible treasuretrove was never out of my mind. As soon as I had my batchelor quarters in an abandoned shed in good order, and my new job in the packinghouse well in hand, I borrowed a shovel, rented a decrepit launch powered by a wheezy single cylinder engine, and set out for a day of treasure hunting.

On a balmy morning in early March I headed down the crooked Estero River to the bay, then nosed my leaking craft towards the distant bulk of Mound Key. I found a landing on a strip of sandy beach, and prepared for a day of digging. At the far end of the strand I saw a fisherman's shantyboat and frames of drying nets, but no sign of life. With shovel, water jug and some sandwiches in a paper bag, I followed a faint jungle path to the base of the mound. Others, I soon discovered, had been there before me. I saw a dozen or more pit marks, some weathered and nearly refilled, while others were no more than a few months old. I selected a spot in the shade of a wild lime tree and began to dig.

The rest of the morning passed quickly. I found many bones and broken pottery, but nothing of any value. My last find of the morning was a human skull with a missing jaw. I balanced the thing on the pile of sand and broken shell removed from the hole, and from there it seemed to watch in hollow-eyed wonder as I ate my meager lunch.

I moved to the far side of the mound in the afternoon, and for a long time I was so interested in my labors that I failed to note a sudden and decided change in the weather. It had become much cooler with a brisk wind from the north, but it was not until a rain squall broke over my head that I hurried back to the beach. One look at the hissing whitecaps of the bay told me that my rented craft would be no mach for the vicious northeaster. I could think of but one thing to do; crouch under my old army poncho until the storm blew over.

Several hours passed. The wind had slowly abated but it was still raining hard when night began to close in. I knew better than to attempt to navigate the twisting and unmarked channels in the dark of a moonless night. With nothing better in view I moved higher on the beach and, with the poncho over my head like a tent, prepared to spend a hungry and miserable night.

Twenty or more minutes went by. The darkness was nearly complete. Suddenly one edge of my poncho lifted. Against the falling murk I could barely make out the form of a girl. Before I could utter more than a surprised "Hello!", she reached down and gripped my wrist.

"Come on, mister!" she shouted above the beat of the cold rain. "Mama says you're to have supper with us."

"Where do you live?" I yelled as I got to my feet.

"There!" She pointed toward the dim lights coming from the distant shantyboat. "Hurry, mister," she pleaded from between chattering teeth, "it's mighty cold out here."

I was in no position to argue. In a bare minute we were stumbling over the uneven sand ridges, with the poncho over our heads and held at the shoulders. When I tripped over a bit of half-buried driftwood her arm was quick to dart around my waist for support. She left it there, and I could feel her slender body shivering from the cold and wet. Her dress was sodden; her hair no more than dripping strings. Guided only by the faint and yellowish glow from two high windows of the shantyboat, we made our way along the shelving beach. The tarred hull loomed before us at last, with the bow end high on the shore and the stern trailing off into shallow water. We climbed a cleated plank to the narrow deck, opened a batten door, and stepped inside.

It was like entering a different world. The interior of the box-like craft was one long room, softly aglow from the light of two oil lamps. The whole of one side of the room was taken up by an old brass bedstead, and a row of double-decked bunks. The opposite side was given over to a cookstove, a nest of shelves heavy with bottles, cans and packages of food, and a long narrow table fitted with two rough plank benches.

It was warm and cozy inside the shantyboat, and the whine of the dying wind and beat of the steady rain came only as a whisper. I heard the laughter of children and sizzle of frying fish. I smelled the aroma of hot corn bread and the fragrance of steaming coffee. I went the length of the room and spoke to the woman tending the stove. She was bare footed, plump and pleasant faced—evidently the mother of the brood. Another woman—at least eighty or over—sat on a stool nearby, with a corn cob pipe clenched in her jaw.

'Thanks for asking me," I said to the younger woman. "Please don't go to any trouble . . . "

"It's no bother, mister," she broke in with a smile. "When you have to feed eight—what's one more? 'Sides, who'd want a person outside on a night like this? Sit at the table, mister—anyplace—supper'll be on in a jiffy."

I sat on a bench, and as I did so I happened to glance to a far corner where all manner of clothing hung from nails driven into the unpainted wall. The girl who had brought me to the houseboat was there, pulling the sodden dress over her head. For a moment she stood there chastely naked with her back to the room, then quickly slipped a dry smock over her shoulders.

It was a meal I'll never forget. Browned pompano, grits, hash browned potatoes, corn bread and molasses, raisin cake and strong coffee with canned milk and brown sugar. While I ate I listened and learned a few facts about this island family. Besides Nancy—the sixteen-year-old who had brought me to the boat, there were five younger children, two girls and three boys, all born on these isolated shores without benefit of doctor, nurse or midwife. I was surprised at the intelligence of the children, and asked where they went to school.

"They don't," the mother replied. "The nearest school's too far, and we can't afford to board them out. 'Sides," she resumed after a moment, "this way they don't learn to lie and cheat and steal—like they would at a school. I'm teaching them all they need to know to grow up decent and respectable. You see, mister, I used to teach country school—up near Cedar Keys—before I up and married in 1900."

I learned something of the father of this family, too. His name was Tobias Butterfield—called Toby for short— and he had gone to Fort Myers the day before to have the engine of his boat overhauled.

While Mrs. Butterfield and the old lady—Toby's mother—cleared the supper away, I watched the girl, Nancy, bathe the two youngest children in a wooden tub, and put them to bed. When the dishes were done Grandmother Butterfield sat beside a lamp, and began reading the fine print of a dog-eared Bible—without glasses. Then Mrs. Butterfield came to sit across the table.

"N-o," she said slowly, in answer to my question, "I wouldn't want to live anywhere else. It's a good place for children. Not a one of mine has ever seen a doctor or dentist. It's good for my man, too—keeps him away from moonshine whiskey most of the time. Oh, he goes on a toot now and then—like his daddy used to do—but it'd be worse if we lived near town and temptation. Toby gets upset sometimes about having to fish so hard for a living. It's times like that when he starts cussing old Adolph Hixson for stealing the fortune Black Augustus left his daddy. I keep telling him it's no use—old Hixson's long dead, and 'sides, the pirate gold had a bad curse on it anyway."

The name, Black Augustus, brought me to quick attention. According to what the garrulous skipper of the *Caloosa Belle* had told me, the half French, half Portuguese pirate had escaped the hangman's noose to finish out his days in hiding on an uncharted key.

"Tell me about Black Augustus — tell me about the gold!" I said, trying to control my eagerness.

"You tell him, Grandma," Mrs. Butterfield directed. "You were with old Black Augustus when he died—he showed you where to find the gold."

The old lady closed her Bible and turned to face me. She was wonderfully preserved. In spite of her years, her sight, hearing and voice were almost perfect. "Me an' Toby's daddy were married soon's he came back from the war in '64," she began. "Toby was most two year old when we came to these parts in a little old sailboat. We set up camp on Sanibel Island first, then moved here to Mound Key. My John—Toby's pappy—he fished, hunted 'gators an' sold egret feathers. Weren't hardly a livin' soul in this whole bay then, 'cept us an' Black Augustus. He had a shack an' a jungle clearing on an island just inside Big Carlos Pass. You could hardly see his face for black whiskers, so we began callin' his place Black Island.

"For the first couple of years," Grandma Butterfield continued, "this Black Augustus used to hide when my John sailed by, then they sort of made up an' began swappin' things. John would give old Augustus a sack of grits, or flour, or sugar, and the old fellow would give John some melons, or a mess of pole beans, okra or squash from his garden in the clearing. The old fellow never went to town — he was still feared they'd hang him for once being a pirate."

The old lady paused to fill her pipe with crumbled raw leaf tobacco. "Things went on that way for twelve-fifteen years," she resumed, blowing a cloud of smoke toward the rafters, "then John began telling me as how old Augustus was gettin' poorly. He was 'bout ninety years old—'cordin' to what he told my John, an' his arms an' legs were beginnin' to stiffen up. It was just plain rheumatism, I 'spose. Anyhow, he kept gettin' worse, 'til near the end he crawled on his elbows an' knees—like an animal, sort of.

"A day came when John left somethin' for old Augustus on the little dock he had, an' the next time he went by

The attack on the MARY ANDERS off Boca Grande in 1820.

it was still there. He went ashore, then, an' found the old man in his shack. Augustus was in his bed of filthy rags, an' mighty near to bein' dead. Bein' a man, my John couldn't do much, but when he got home an' told me 'bout it we left the young'uns with Toby—he was 'bout nineteen then—an' I made John take me over to Black Island.''

Grandmother paused to relight her pipe above the lamp chimney. "I washed Augustus the best I could," she continued, "an' put him 'tween some blankets I'd taken along. He was unconscious and mumblin' some kind of foreign talk. We could see he was goin' to go 'most any minute an' there wasn't any use even tryin' to get a doctor. Sure enough, he died 'bout an hour after I got there, an' we buried him beside his garden patch.

"It was strange to see, mister," Grandmother Butterfield went on, "but just 'fore he died his good sense seemed to come back for just a minute. His eyes were open, an' he was tryin' to tell me somethin', but his tongue was so thick he couldn't talk. Then, while I watched, he took all the strength he had left an' pointed to a corner of the dirt floor. He made a couple weak motions—like diggin' with a scoop, then fell back an' closed his eyes. I heard a rattle in his throat, an' in another minute he was gone.

"After we had him buried we went back to the shack an' dug up the floor where he'd pointed. Do you know what we found, mister?" I shook my head. "Well," she continued, "it was a lump 'bout the size of a big grapefruit, an' real, real heavy. John scratched the stuff an' it showed the same color as my weddin' ring. That's how we knew it must be gold. John said it looked like it had been melted down in a blacksmith's forge. We dug up the rest of the floor after that, but weren't anything more."

The old lady sighed at the memory. "That night," she continued, "we talked about what to do with the money we'd get for the gold. John said he'd get a better boat an' some new nets, an' we made plans to send Toby away to learn a good trade—so he wouldn't need to fish all his life. If there was enough left over we planned to get things for the younger children, an' maybe a new cook stove for me."

The old lady emptied her pipe into a mussel shell on the table, and leaned back. "John said he'd take the gold to town in the morning, an' show it to Mr. Hixson. Old Adolph Hixson's been dead a long time now, mister, but he used to run a general store an' carry a lot of the fishermen on his books when the catch was runnin' poor. So that's what John did. He sailed off in the mornin' with the lump wrapped in flour sacks, an' hid away in the stern locker. I didn't see my John again for most of two weeks."

Again I had to wait until Grandmother Butterfield re-filled and lit her pipe. A quietness settled over the shanty-boat. All the children were in their bunks save the girl, Nancy. She was combing her hair in front of a cracked mirror nailed to an upright, and almost lost in the folds of a bulky nightgown.

"When John showed the lump to Mr. Hixson," the old lady resumed, "the storekeeper dug it with his knife an' matched the color with his watch chain. Then he put it on his scales an' said he'd have to send it to the bank in Tampa to see what it would bring. He gave John ten dollars an' a jug of store whiskey, an' told him he could stay in the back room of the store 'til they found out what the bank said. Of course, mister, Old Adolph knew John would stay drunk long as the money an' whiskey lasted. Drinkin' was John's only bad habit. God bless his poor soul, an' he didn't do it often.

"I 'spect you can guess what happened, mister," the old lady smiled sadly. "When John gets his good sense back—after 'bout ten days—Adolph Hixson tells him the Tampa bank said the lump was nothin' but melted brass— worth maybe two or three dollars. Then old Hixson gave John ten more dollars—out of the goodness of his heart, he said—an' sent John home to me." The old lady laid her pipe on the oil cloth covered table and sighed. "So you see, mister, that's what happened to the stuff Augustus left us —gold or brass, whatever it was."

"But you're sure it was gold," I suggested.

Grandmother Butterfield s h r u g g e d her shoulders. "Must have been," she agreed, "for soon after that old Hixson built a new store—twice as big—an' put in a lot of new stock. Next he had his home painted an' put on a porch. Then, come September, he sent his girl, Ethel, off to some fancy college, an' come Christmas he ordered his wife one of those play-organs—like they use in church. The way most of the town people figured, the lump had to be gold."

Silence again fell over the room. I cast a quick glance around the humble home and few possession of the Butterfield tribe. When I began to express sympathy for the scurvy trick fate had played on them, the old lady cut me short.

"Don't take on 'bout it, mister," she interrupted. "It was hard for me an' John to take at first, but after a couple years went by—why, we was glad old Hixson stole the pirate's gold. Yes," she sighed, "I'm sorry 'bout what happened to him, but it was better him than us."

The old lady was getting ahead of me, and I didn't understand. "Why," I asked, "are you sorry for Hixson, but glad he stole the gold?"

" 'Cause there was blood on that gold, that's why. There's a curse put on pirate gold by the souls of the innocent folks they'd robbed and murdered. You take my word, mister, evil happens to anybody who tries to spend it."

"Then something must have happened to this Hixson?" I suggested.

The old lady nodded and picked up her pipe. " 'Bout a year after he stole the gold his wife, Carrie, went out on the City Dock at night, took off her clothes, and' drowned herself in the Caloosahatchee. The next year his girl, Ethel, was found stabbed to death in some fellow's hotel room up in Georgia. A couple years later—it was about 1890—old Hixson's store burned up without any insurance. A couple months later his house burned up, an' the next day they found his body in the ashes, with a shotgun in his arms, an' one side of his head blowed off. You see now, mister, why I say there's a curse on pirate gold!"

The slave auction at Santiago De Cuba in 1795

This Spanish piece-of-eight, often called a Spanish dollar, is slightly larger than a U.S. silver dollar. Many millions of them were coined in Mexico and shipped to Spain in the 1700's and 1800's. This specimen was found in a mound on Fort Myers Beach, along with other coins and gold and silver jewelry. There were also pieces-of-four, pieces-of-two and single pieces, and from this old coinage comes our slang terms of two bits, four bits and six bits.

For a minute the silence was broken only by the faint patter of the dwindling rain on the tarpaper roof. I could think of nothing to say. Then I noticed the younger Mrs. Butterfield yawning. I got up to leave. I hated the thought of spending a miserable night under the damp folds of my clammy poncho, but what else could I do? I began to thank Mrs. Butterfield for her wonderful hospitality, but when she discovered my intent to go back to the beach, she would not hear of it.

"You're not going to sleep outside a night like this," she said sharply. "What kind of folks do you think we are? I'll wake Nancy and have her sleep with me. You can have her bunk."

"But—but your husband . . . ?" I stammered.

"He'd want you to stay," she insisted. "It's all right— there's no use talking about it. Besides—you've got a good face, and I've got a pistol. Now you'll want to go outside first—you can blow out the lamp when you come back in. Hope you sleep good, mister."

The girl, Nancy, was in the brass bedstead with her mother when I returned from the wet and cold of the night. All I could hear was the tap of the rain and the breathing of children caught in their dreams. I removed my coat, shirt and shoes, blew out the lamp, and crawled gratefully into Nancy's bunk. It was still warm from the animal heat of her young healthy body. I was soon asleep, but before I dozed off I gave silent thanks that the curse of pirate's gold had not been visited upon the simple, kindly and warm-hearted Butterfield family.

The Capture of the 'Mary Anders' Off Boca Grande in 1820

Note: This is an almost word-for-word account of pirate brutality as published in the *American Monthly Magazine* in the February, 1824, issue. It was printed under the title "PIRACY", and the name of the author was not given.

"In the early part of June, 1820, I sailed from my home in Philadelphia in the schooner *Mary Anders*, on a voyage to new Orleans. My principle object in going around by sea was the restoration of my health, which had been for many months declining. Having some friends in New Orleans whose commercial operations were conducted on an extensive scale, I was charged with the care of several sums of money in gold and silver, amounting to nearly eighteen thousand dollars. This fact I at once communicated to the captain, and we concluded to secure it in the best manner our circumstances would permit.

"A plank was accordingly taken up from the ribs of the schooner in my own cabin, and the money being deposited in the vacancy, the plank was nailed down to its original place, and the seams filled and tarred over. Being thus relieved from any apprehension that the money would be found upon us in case of attack by pirates, my mind was made much easier. What other articles of value I could conveniently carry about with me, I did so.

"I had brought a quantity of bank notes to the amount of fifteen thousand dollars. Part of these I caused to be carefully sewed in the left lapel of my coat, supposing that in case of my being lost at sea, my coat, should my body be found, would still contain the most valuable of my effects. The balance of the notes were carefully quilted into my black silk cravat.

"Our crew consisted of the Captain and four men, with a supply of live stock for the voyage, and a Newfoundland dog, valuable for his fidelity and sagacity. He had once saved his master from a watery grave, when he had been stunned and knocked overboard by a sudden shifting of the boom. I was the only passenger on board. Our voyage at first was prosperous, and time went on rapidly. I felt my strength increase the longer I was at sea, and when we arrived off the southern coast of Florida, my feelings were those of another man.

"It was towards the evening of the fourteenth day, two hours before sunset, that we espied a sail astern of us. We were in the Gulf of Mexico, and adverse winds had kept us far east of where a normal course would have led us, so that we were no more than thirty or forty miles from the many islands that fringe the Florida shore, and which reports say are the hiding places of several pirate bands.

"As twilight came, the strange vessel neared us with astonishing speed. Night closed, and all around us was impenetrable darkness. Now and then a gentle wave would break against our bow, and sparkle for a moment, and at a distance behind us, we could see the uneven glow of light, occasioned by the foaming bow wave of the strange vessel. The breeze that filled our sails blew first fresh then gentle.

"We coursed our way steadily through the night; though once or twice the roaring of the waves increased so suddenly, as to make us believe we had passed a breaker. At the time it was unaccountable to me, but now I believe it to have been occasioned by the bark behind us, coming near in the blackness of the night. At midnight I went on deck. Nothing but an occasional sparkle was to be seen, and the ocean was undisturbed. Still it was a fearful and appalling darkness, and in spite of my endeavors I could not compose myself that all was well.

"At the windlass on the forecastle, three of the sailors like myself, unable to sleep, had collected for conversation. On joining them, I found our fears were mutual. The sailors had heard true and horrible tales of a pirate called Gasparilla, and others of like ilk, who inhabited some of the larger islands on the wild coast of Florida. I noticed the sailors all kept their gaze steadily fixed toward the unknown vessel, as if anticipating some dreadful event. They informed me that they had put the ship's arms in order, and where determined to stand or die.

"At this moment a flash of light, perhaps a musket burning the priming, proceeded from the vessel in pursuit, and we saw distinctly that her deck was covered with men. My heart almost failed me. I had never been in battle, and I knew not what it was like. Day at length dawned, and setting all her canvass, our pursuer gained alarmingly upon us. It was evident that she had followed us the whole night, being unwilling to attack us in the dark.

"In a few minutes the black hulled vessel fired her swivel gun, and then came along side. That she was a pirate there was no single doubt. Her boat was lowered, and about a dozen hideous looking rascals jumped in, with a commander in the stern seat. The boat pushed off, and was nearing us fast, as we arranged ourselves for giving the small boat a broadside. Our whole stock of arms consisted of six muskets and an old swivel used as a signal gun, belonging to the *Mary Anders*, and a pair of pistols of my own which I carried in my belt.

"As the pirate boat neared I could see they were armed with muskets, pistols, swords, cutlasses, and knives. We waited until they were within one length of us, then fired five of our muskets and the old swivel gun at point blank range. Her fire was scarce half returned when she filled and went down with all her crew. At this sudden success we were inclined to rejoice, but looking over at the pirate schooner, we observed her deck still swarming with the same description of horrible looking wretches.

"Within minutes a second boat's crew pushed away, with their muskets pointing directly at us the whole time. Then they came within the same distance as the first boat, we fired, but this time with little, if any effect. The pirates immediately returned the fire, and with hideous cries jumped aboard of us.

'I took time to glance down at our deck. Two of our brave crew were already dead at our feet, and the rest of us expected nothing better. The pirates kept up a constant howling. French, Spanish and English were spoken indiscriminately, and all at once. The most horrid imprecations were uttered against us, and threats that fancy can hardly imagine.

"I took particular notice of the wretch who seemed to be in charge of the attack upon us. Black, shaggy whiskers covered nearly his whole face, and his eyes could only be seen at intervals from beneath his bushy eyebrows. One of his men called him by name, Augustus, and his whole appearance was more that of a hell-hound than a human being. He came at me with a naked cutlass in his huge fist. I drew one of my pistols and snapped it in his face; but it flashed in the pan, and before I could draw the other, the pirate, with a brutality that would have disgraced a cannibal, struck me over the face with his cutlass, and knocked me down.

"I was too much wounded by the blow to resist, and the blood ran in torrents from my forehead. In this situation the vile brute seized me by the scalp, and thrusting his cutlass in my cravat, cut it through completely. I felt the cold steel glide across my thoat, and even now the very thought makes me shudder. The worst idea I had ever formed of depraved human cruelty seemed now realized, and I could see death stare me in the face. Without stopping to examine the severed cravat, he put it in his pocket, and in a voice of thunder exclaimed, *"Levez vous!"* I understood some French and accordingly got to my feet.   The villian next pinioned my hands behind my back, led me to the gunwale of the vessel, and asked another of the gang, in French, if it would be a good idea to throw me overboard.

"At the recollection of that scene I am still staggered. I endeavoured to call the prospects of eternity before me, but could think of nothing but the cold and quiverless apathy of the tomb. His infamous companion replied, *"Il ne vaut pas peine de le sauver, envoyez le au diable!"*, and led me to the foremast. There I was tied with my face to the stern of the vessel. The cords were drawn so tight around my arms and legs, that the agony I suffered was excruciating. In this situation they left me.

"On looking around as best I might I found all the pirates employed in plundering and ransacking everything aboard. Over my left shoulder I saw one of our sailors strung up to the yard arm, and apparently in the last agonies of death; while before me our gallant captain was on his knees and begging for his life. The wretches were endeavouring to extort from him the secret hiding place of our money; but for awhile he was firm and dauntless, and would tell nothing they wanted to know.

"Provoked at last at the Captain's obstinacy, they extended his arms and, with several blows of a cutlass, severed them at the elbows. At this human nature gave way, and the injured man confessed the spot where we had concealed the bags of coins. In a few minutes the gold and silver coinage was hauled aboard the pirate vessel.

"The inhuman monsters, when they had satisfied themselves that nothing else was there hidden, returned to revenge themselves on the dying captain. They prepared a bed of oakum on the foredeck, and after soaking it through with turpentine, tied the Captain on it, filled his mouth with the same combustibles, and set the whole on fire. The cries of the unfortunate man were heartrending, and the agonies must have been unutterable, but were soon over.

"All this I was compelled to witness. Heart-sick at the sight, I once shut my eyes, but a pirate discharged a musket close to my ear, and it was a sufficient warning to keep them open. When I next looked to the stern, I discovered the boatswain had been nailed to the deck through his feet, and his body spiked through to the tiller. He was writhing in the last agonies of crucifixion.

"Our fifth comrade was out of sight during all this tragedy. In a few minutes, however, he was dragged into my sight with a blindfold over his eyes. I saw him conducted to the muzzel of our swivel gun, where he was commanded to kneel. The swivel was then fired at his head, and he was dreadfully wounded by the discharge. In the moments after it was agonizing to behold his torments and convulsions—language is too feeble to describe them. I have seen men hung from the gibbet, but their death was like sinking into sweet slumber when compared to this.

"Excited with this scene of human butchery, one of the wretches fired his pistol at the Captain's dog. The ball struck the shoulder and disabled the poor animal, but the pirate finished by shooting the dog again, and then, with his dagger, carved out the brute's tongue. At this last hell-engendered act my blood boiled with indignation at such savagery on a helpless, inoffensive dog, but I was unable to give utterance or action to my feelings.

"Realizing that every member of the crew had been dispatched, I began to think of my own life. My old enemy, the hairy brute they called Augustus, who had seemed to have forgotten me for a time, once more approached me. I saw he was shockingly smeared with blood and brains. He had been beside the unfortunate sailor who suffered death from the swivel gun, supporting the doomed sailor with his sword when the charge was fired. Now he drew a stiletto from his side, placed the point over my heart and gave it a heavy thrust. I felt the point pierce my skin, but the quilting of my bank bills prevented its further entrance.

"This savage monster then ran the knife blade up my breast, as if intending to divide my lungs, and in so doing the wad of bank notes fell upon the deck. He snatched them up greedily, and exclaimed, *"Laissez moi voir ce qui reste!"* I answered that I had nothing left of value, but he proceeded to cut my clothes apart at the peril of my life. His blade frequently came so near as to split my skin and deluge me with blood, but by the Mercy of Providence I escaped from this danger. I next heard a pirate shout in English that Gasparilla was signaling for them to return to the pirate ship, and a minute after I heard blows being struck down in the hold. Then one of the pirates yelled, *"Voila un vaisseau!"*—a ship is coming—and they all ran to their boat and rowed toward their vessel. Soon they were hull down, veering to the east and the islands of the Florida coast.

"Helpless as I now was, I had the satistfaction of knowing that the pirates had been frightened by the appearance of a sail, but it was impossible for me to see it. I alone lived aboard the *Mary Anders*, and I saw no prospect of release from the ropes binding me to the mast. An hour or two had elapsed since the departure of the pirates, and by the shadow of the sun I could tell it was nearing noon. The sun played violently on my head, and I felt a languor and debility that indicated approaching fever. My head gradually sank upon my breast for I was weak from apprehension and loss of blood. I knew little more until I was shocked into wakefulness by the sound of water pouring in the cabin windows below.

The vile wretches had scuttled the vessel, and left me pinioned to go down with her.

"I commended my Spirit to my Maker, and gave myself up for lost. I felt myself gradually dying away, and the last thing I remember was the noise of foaming water coming closer—ever closer. This I slowly discovered was occasioned by a ship approaching from the port quarter. Almost unconscious to my remaining fate in this world, I felt myself being lifted into a small boat. Then I knew no more for some time.

"I was cared for very well by my saviors, who came just in time to spare me for a longer span of life upon this wicked sphere. I am now well restored to health in body, but my mind suffers from permanent scars from what I have seen, and I remain a poor, ruined and helpless man."

When Pirates Roamed
Pine Island Sound

Little is known about the early life of Brewster Baker, save that he was born about 1758 in, or near, the town of Avonmouth on the Bristol Channel in the south of England. His father ran a grog shop patronized by sailors, and the boy heard many a tale of the sea, pirates, and strange lands and people. He learned to sail on the River Severn, and at the age of fifteen he joined the navy to sample some of the adventures he had heard from the lips of seafarers.

The *Pirates' Who's Who*, an old English book which is the Bible of the pirates' trade, gives very little of young Baker's life, save to say that he was "one of Gasparilla's gang up to 1820", and that "his favorite hunting ground was the Gulf of Mexico."

In the year 1780, when he was twenty-two, we find him among the crew of H.M.S. *Warnock*, a frigate of 24 guns. By this time he had become a midshipman, and about two years later, while the *Warnock* was in the neutral port of Fort de France, on the French Island of Martinique, he met the young captain of a Spanish man-of-war. His new found friend was none other than José Gaspar, skipper of the *Alborada,* and they became fast friends even though they were far apart in rank.

Both officers had something in common, for they were making violent love to the two daughters of a wealthy planter of the island. Of course neither man had any intention of taking a wife—when there were so many West Indian isles with so many young ladies willing and waiting. It was the old game "of a girl in every port—and why settle for less?" Still the pursuit of the two French *mademoiselles* tended to cement the friendship of the navy officers, and it was to last through many years.

Nothing much is now known of Brewster Baker's remaining years in His Majesty's service, save that he gradually changed the spelling of his name to Brew Baker, and later to Bru Baker, and received promotions with ordinary regularity.

In 1797 we find him aboard H.M.S. *Heather,* a brig of 14 guns, anchored in the bight at Bridgeton, on the Island of Barbados in the Lesser Antilles. He was Lieutenant Baker by this time, but for some reason he led a mutiny, put the loyal members of the crew ashore, and sailed away as the captain of the ship, and with piracy in mind. Sometime later he captured a splendid French ship, the *Andre Follet,* at the French Island of Guadeloupe, and began to prey on likely ships of any nation, and the risks seeming not too great.

In some manner not known he had become aware of the piratical exploits of his old friend, José Gaspar—now becoming well known as "Gasparilla"—and he decided to join forces with the great Gaspar, and to become one of the "Captains of the Brotherhood of the Seas". With this in mind he set sail for Charlotte Harbor and, under a white flag of truce, he sailed into Boca Grande Pass and made his identity known.

What the two pirate captains talked about is not known, but meet they did, and an agreement was duly signed and sealed. For a short time Bru Baker berthed the *Andre Follet* with Gasparilla's ships at Boca Grande, but the arrangement left a lot to be desired. Before long Baker's English crew were at war with Gaspar's mixed and motley crew of Spaniards, Portuguese, French and half-breed buccaneers. Men from both sides were knifed or murdered, but Bru Baker's men were sadly outnumbered, and he was forced to act.

Being forced to move his ship and men from Boca Grande, yet still being satisfied to work hand-in-glove with Gasparilla, Captain Baker looked for a more healthy berth for himself and his crew. The place he finally chose for his shore camp was a small island at the head of Pine Island, a place the Spaniards had named Bojelia, but which Bru Baker's men changed to Bokeelia. Here on this bit of land thatched huts were built, and a place for careening the vessel was established.

About the year 1800 Bru Baker fell in with one of the privateers belonging to the Brothers La Fitte of New Orleans, and it was through this meeting that Gasparilla was able to arrange the sale of much valuable plunder to the dishonest merchants at Barataria, on the Louisiana coast.

When, in 1819, rumors gave the news that the United States was about to purchase all of Florida from Spain, Captain Baker saw the handwirtng on the wall. He had no wish to buck his small strength against the might of the U.S. Navy. Instead he desired to gather his wealth from the island hiding places, and start a new and better life in one of the new countries in South or Central America. He arranged a final division of the spoils of piracy with Gasparilla, and left Florida waters for good.

If history can be depended upon, Bru Baker met a sad, but perhaps well deserved fate. The *Andre Follet* sailed from Charlotte Harbor about the end of November, 1820, and headed for the new Republic of Columbia. His declared intention was to settle down as a retired gentlemen, or else to join the army of Simon Bolivar, and help free the whole continent of Spanish rule.

Instead of reaching Cartagena as planned, Captain Baker went ashore at a native village on the Gulf of Darien for some reason, and was attacked by naked Indians. A poisoned arrow in his chest brought hours of agony, and then death. Whether he left any treasure at Bokeelia—or on Pine Island—is not known for certain, but there have been rumors of rich "finds".

List of Atrocious Piracies
and Barbarities

Author's Note: *The following stories have been taken from newspaper accounts as published in Boston, Massachusetts, in the early 1800s.*

Boston, Nov. 6, 1821.

The brig. *Cobbessecontee*, Capt. Jackson, arrived yesterday from Havana. About four miles from Morro Castle she was attacked by a piratical sloop, containing about 30 men. A boat with ten men came alongside, and as soon as they were aboard they began plundering. They took nearly all the clothing of the Captain and mate—all the cooking utensils and spare rigging—unrove part of the running rigging—cut the small cable—broke the compasses—cut the mate's coat to pieces—took from the Captain his watch and four boxes of cigars—and from the cargo three bales of cochineal and six cases of cigars. They beat the mate unmercifully, and hung him by the neck under the maintop. They also beat the Captain severely—broke a large broad sword across his back, and ran a long knife through his thigh, so that he almost bled to death. Capt. Jackson had seen the sloop in port the day before.

Capt. Jackson informs us, and we have also been informed by other persons from the Havana, that this system of Piracy is openly countenanced by the authorities of that place—who say it is a retaliation on the Americans for interfering against the Slave Trade, and for allowing Patriot privateers to refit in their ports. The pirates, therefore, receiving such countenance, grow more daring—and increase in numbers from the success which has attended this new mode of filling their pockets.

Capt. Bugnon, who arrived yesterday from Charleston, spoke on the 2d inst. off the S. Shoal of Nantucket, the brig *Three Partners,* from Jamaica for St. John—which had been robbed off Cape Antonio, by a piratical vessel, of about 35 tons, and 17 men, of clothing, watches, etc., and the captain was hung by the neck to the fore-yard arm, till he was almost dead.

The brig *Harriet,* Capt. Dimond, from St. Jago de Cuba for Baltimore, arrived at Havana on the 16th ult. having been robbed of all her cargo of sugar, and $4000 in specie, off Cape Antonio, by a boat with 15 men, having two schooners in company. Capt. Dimond was hung up by the neck, and remained senseless for some time after he was taken down.

The Dutch brig *Mercury* arrived on the 16th ult. after having been robbed of $10,000 worth of her cargo, by a piratical schooner and boat, off Cape Antonio, Cuba.

Fortunately a U. S. vessel has arrived at the scene of these daring robberies, and has already protected several American vessels.

A letter from a gentleman aboard the U. S. Brig *Spark*, dated at St. Barts, Nov. 3, 1827, says—

"We arrived here, after a rather rough passage, in eighteen days from Boston, all well. We expect to sail again in two or three days. We found here the piratical ship which robbed the Orleans Packet. All but two of the pirate crew had deserted the vessel, which was originally the U.S. Brig *Prometheus,* which was condemned two years since, and had been sold. Our captain has requested the Governor to allow him to take these two pirates to the United States for trial."

A letter from on board the Hornet, dated at Cape Maise, Cuba, 31st, October, says, "The pirate which we took yesterday mounted two long four pounders, and her crew consisted of twenty callous—-looking scoundrels. After this capture the Hornet spoke three merchant brigs, which probably would have fallen into the hands of other pirates, and they escaped."

Charleston, Jan. 16, 1822.

The *Porpoise,* Capt. Ramage, arrived at Charleston from a successful cruise against the Pirates, having recaptured a Baltimore schooner which had been in their possession three days, destroying three of their establishments on shore, 12 of their vessels, besides two on the stocks, and brought in four prisoners, against whom it is supposed there is strong evidence.

It is stated, that a Pirate Captain and his mate quarrelled on the question of putting to death all captives, and fought a duel with muskets. The Captain was killed, and the Mate (who was the advocate of mercy) succeeded to the command.

If the Spanish Government is unable to drive the Pirates from their strong holds in Cuba, the Baltimore Chronicle suggests the necessity of occupying the island with American forces for that purpose, as robbers and pirates have a right to enjoy no protection whatever; and in this case all civilized powers are warranted in carrying the war into the enemy's territory.

Baltimore, Jan. 17, 1823.

Yesterday Commodore Porter left this port in the steam galley *Enterprise,* to join the squadron fitted out at Norfolk, for the purpose of suppressing piracy on the coast of Cuba. Sailing frigates and sloops-of-war are totally inadequate, by means of their great draft of water; but the steam vessels which have been selected by Commodore Porter are precisely calculated to ferret the banditti from their lurking places. The aid of steam we think a most valuable addition to the squadron, and from the manner in which the *Enterprise* has been fitted out, we have every reason to believe she will completely answer the expectations formed.

In a very short time we hope the Commodore will soon put an end to the ravages of those lawless barbarians.